LUCY PARSONS

FREEDOM, EQUALITY & SOLIDARITY

Writings & Speeches, 1878-1937

Edited & Introduced by
GALE AHRENS

with an Afterword by
ROXANNE DUNBAR-ORTIZ

T0315229

Revolutionary Classics

CHICAGO
CHARLES H. KERR PUBLISHING COMPANY
Established 1886
2004

© Copyright 2023
Charles H. Kerr Publishing Company
charleshkerr.com

This work is licensed under a Creative Commons BY-NC-SA
license. This license allows readers to distribute, remix, adapt,
and build upon the material in any medium or format (1) for
noncommercial purposes only, (2) only so long as attribution is
given to the creator, and (3) only with notification to Charles H.
Kerr Publishing Company in writing via postal mail or email. If
you remix, adapt, or build upon the material, you must license
the modified material under identical terms.

ISBN 978-0-88286-012-1

Cover art by "Copyright Is for Losers"

WANTED

For future publishing projects:
Photos, publications, artwork, memorabilia, and ephemera
concerning the IWW, anarchism, the early Socialist Party,
Bughouse Square, Hobo College, the Dil Pickle Club,
other free-speech forums,
and early Charles H. Kerr publications.
Please write to us at
charleshkerrpublishing@gmail.com.

CHARLES H. KERR PUBLISHING COMPANY
Established 1886
8901 South Exchange Avenue, First Floor
Chicago, Illinois 60617

This book
is dedicated to
ALMA WASHINGTON
whose wonderful performances as
LUCY PARSONS
(starting in 1986)
have brought Lucy's brave spirit
and bold words
to wide attention.

Illinois Labor History Society

Alma Washington continues
to portray Lucy Parsons at
schools, union events, and
many other venues. For further
information contact the
Illinois Labor History Society
312-341-2247 or
ilaborhistorys@gmail.com

ON THE TEXTS IN THIS BOOK

This selection of the writings and speeches of Lucy Parsons opens with her only pamphlet, *The Principles of Anarchism*, the precise publication date of which is not known. The other texts appear in chronological order.

Like most speakers on tour, Lucy Parsons often inserted parts of old speeches into new ones. Many texts here have therefore been edited, and indicated as such in the source-notes.

Spanning nearly sixty years, these writings reflect changes in style and usage. In the early texts, Lucy freely used such terms as *capitalistic* and *anarchistic*; later she adopted the modern forms: *capitalist* and *anarchist*. These and other minor inconsistencies should not prove troublesome to the reader. Obvious misspellings have been corrected, and punctuation modernized.

The 1930 Chicago May Day speech, the 1934 letter to Carl Nold, and the 1937 message of solidarity to the IWW's General Defense Committee are, to the best of our knowledge, published here for the first time.

Some names and topics that may be unfamiliar to today's readers are flagged with an asterisk (*) and identified in the "Notes to the Texts" on page 167.

ACKNOWLEDGMENTS

Special thanks to Roxanne Dunbar-Ortiz for her fine Afterword; to Kenan Heise for providing the transcript of Lucy's 1930 May Day speech; to Carlos Cortez for the 1937 message to the IWW's General Defense Committee; and to Franklin Rosemont for sharing his own Lucy Parsons research.

Thanks also to Alex Dodge, Paul Garon, Anne Olson, Ruth Oppenheim-Rothschild, Constance Rosemont, Penelope Rosemont and Meg Whedbee for various kinds of technical assistance.

And thanks to the many librarians who helped on this project, especially to Diana Haskell at The Newberry Library in Chicago; Julie Herrada, Labadie Collection, University of Michigan, Ann Arbor; Martha Quinn, Evanston Public Library; and the always helpful staff of the Illinois Labor History Society, caretakers of the Haymarket Martyrs' Monument at Forest Home Cemetery in Forest Park, IL.

TABLE OF CONTENTS

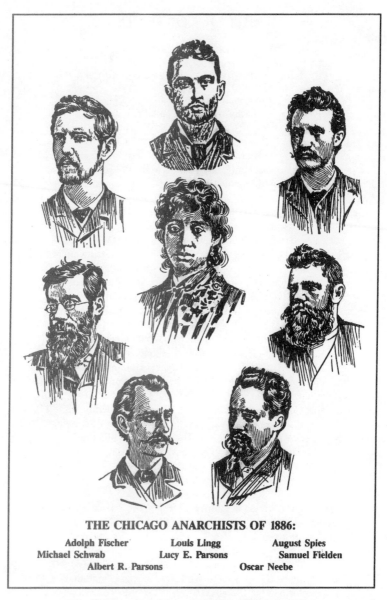

THE CHICAGO ANARCHISTS OF 1886:

Adolph Fischer   Louis Lingg   August Spies
Michael Schwab   Lucy E. Parsons   Samuel Fielden
Albert R. Parsons   Oscar Neebe

The Chicago Anarchists of 1886: A 1901 engraving

GALE AHRENS

INTRODUCTION

Lucy Parsons: Mystery Revolutionist, More Dangerous Than a Thousand Rioters

Free spirit, anarchist, socialist, revolutionist, union organizer, agitator, speaker, writer, editor, publisher, and inspirer of three generations of radicals from the late 1870s through the early 1940s, Lucy Parsons was widely known in her own time but is far from a familiar name today, never featured on TV or in supermarket tabloids. Historians and journalists alike have long conspired, perhaps unwittingly, to reduce her important place in our history. "Best known as wife-partner-defender-widow of Haymarket Martyr Albert Parsons" is the identification generally applied to her, but it simply isn't enough. "Best known as" does far too little to describe the range and power of this amazing force of nature whose life of struggle and defiance does far more to define the vital issues of her time (and ours) than any and all of the billionaire industrialists or their presidents, senators, generals, and other assorted celebrity yes-men of the day.

As Robin D. G. Kelley put it so well in his *Freedom Dreams: The Black Radical Imagination* (2002), Lucy Parsons was not only "the most prominent black woman radical of the late nineteenth century," but also "one of the brightest lights in the history of revolutionary socialism."[1]

The purpose of the present volume is to make available, for the first time in book-form, the ideas and opinions of Lucy Parsons *in her own words*. Considering how famous she was in her life-time—or notorious, if you prefer, for she always was and remains controversial—it is incredible that no selection of her writings and speeches has appeared before this. The Charles H. Kerr Publishing Company has long sought to recover the "lost voices" of American radicalism, and this collection is an important contribution to that worthy project.

The far-ranging writings and speeches gathered here give the lie to those who have attempted to soften the sting of Lucy Parsons's burning truths by pretending that she was merely the shadow of her martyred husband. These texts are representative of Lucy's constant themes as writer and lecturer from her young womanhood to her last years. Included are a few pre-Haymarket writings, articles on the Haymarket events and the infamous show-trial, several general pieces on anarchism in theory and practice, and all of her writings related to the Industrial Workers of the World (IWW) that we were able to find. Of particular interest —especially because most commentators have ignored them entirely—are her articles on women, on the oppression of people of color, on child labor, and on crime. Also included are a couple of her prefaces to books she published, a few letters, and her only known work of fiction: a proletarian Christmas story.

In the Afterword to this book, activist/historian Roxanne Dunbar-Ortiz reflects on Lucy Parsons's revolutionary ideas and activities, as well as her diverse legacies for radical social movements in our own time. In contrast, this introductory essay is primarily biographical, focused on what little is known of Lucy Parsons's life, with a few bits of information heretofore overlooked in the literature about her. Along the way I discuss the interacting milieux in which she lived and worked, and examine some of the dubious legends that continue to cluster around her.

* * *

Speculation and rumor surround the life and memory of Lucy Parsons—which comes as no surprise at all. Like many other workingclass radicals of those years—Joe Hill is a classic example —she never liked to talk about herself; she felt that it was the revolutionary movement that was all-important, not the individual. "The cause," she liked to say, "is above you and me." She was glad to discuss major events and struggles in which she had taken part, but had no time for "biography" as such. Her admirers were many, but they respected her privacy; no one ever seems to have attempted an oral history of Lucy Parsons.

Further clouding the issue of biography is the fact that the forces of "law'n'order" seized Lucy Parsons's papers at the time of her death, and most likely destroyed and/or "disappeared" them in order to silence her history and her voice in the ash-heap of repression. The only book-length biography, Carolyn Ashbaugh's *Lucy Parsons: American Revolutionary*, published by Charles H. Kerr in 1976, has the virtues as well as the weaknesses of many pioneering studies. Ashbaugh's enthusiasm for Lucy is evident throughout, and she assembled a mass of facts as well as interesting quotations from interviews and/or correspondence with old-timers who actually knew Lucy Parsons. Nearly three decades later, the book is still the central source on the subject. Unfortunately, it suffers from oversimplification—especially in regard to the complex problems regarding Lucy's ethnic origins. By simply declaring Lucy black, Ashbaugh too casually disregards Lucy's own repeated assertions that she was at least partly Mexican and Native American. And when she touches on the theories of the different schools of anarchism, and their relation to Marxism and the IWW, Ashbaugh is often superficial and condescending. One of the worst things about the book is her habit of referring to the Haymarket anarchists as "anarchists"—*i. e.*, in quotation marks, as if these men who went to their deaths on the scaffold shouting "Long Live Anarchy!" weren't truly anarchists at all!

Regrettable, too, is Ashbaugh's heavy reliance on hearsay. Too much of her book is drawn from daily newspapers—publications that regularly receive but rarely deserve this sort of credibility. Worse yet is her careless passing remark that Lucy was a member of the Communist Party—a statement for which there appears to be no evidence whatsoever.

In more ways than one Lucy Parsons remains a woman of mystery—a mystery revolutionist.

* * *

Almost nothing is known about Lucy Parsons's early life; even her maiden name is disputed. When she lived with Oliver Gaithings (prior to her meeting Albert Parsons) she used the surname Gaithings. Over the years she used many different last names (including Carter, Hull, Diaz, and Gonzales) when filling out various bureaucratic forms. Her middle name is also an open question.

3

She almost always signed her name Lucy E. Parsons, but whether the E is for Ella or Eldine depends on which document you happen to consult. Way to go, Lucy! What a grand gesture against bureaucrats who consign our lives to paperwork and numbers!

Regarding the first twenty years of her life, mostly what we have are questions. Did she even know who her parents were, most especially her father? When and where did she learn to write and read? And what did she read? Was she fluent in Spanish? And how did she become a radical? What drove her to revolutionary fervor, to abandon conformity for dreams most people consider impossible, dangerous, quixotic, utopian?

The few more or less verifiable facts about her early years can be told in a few paragraphs. Lucy Parsons was born *circa* 1853 in Waco, Texas. Considering the time and place of her birth, and the fact that Oliver Gaithings, with whom she had lived, was a former slave, it is virtually certain that she herself was born into slavery. The records seem to indicate that she was indeed of "mixed" descent—African American, Mexican, Native American.

She witnessed the Civil War as a pubescent child, and as a teenager lived through its horrendous Texas aftermath, including Ku Klux Klan atrocities. Sometime between 1869 and 1871, in Waco, she met Albert Parsons, a young printer and former Confederate army scout who had become a radical and taken up the cause of Reconstruction and Radical Republicanism, including black suffrage. They married (officially or not) in 1871 or 72, in Austin, and moved to Chicago in 73 or early 74.

In Chicago they settled into the poor German immigrant neighborhood on the North Side. Although they had to move frequently, for political and other reasons, they mostly lived in the vicinity of North Avenue and Larrabee Streets in Lincoln Park—today one of the most gentrified areas of the city.[2] In Chicago at least they didn't have to worry about terrorist attacks by the Ku Klux Klan.

Within a year or two of their arrival in Chicago Albert and Lucy were both active in the city's radical Workingmen's Party, and not long afterward were writing articles for the *Socialist*, organ of the Socialistic Labor Party (SLP). Albert joined Chicago Typographical Union No. 16 and soon became one of its most prominent and widely respected members—and indeed, one of the most

4

influential figures in the Chicago labor movement. The 1870s and 80s were years of intensified class struggle all over the U.S., especially in Chicago, and the Parsonses were in the thick of it. The huge nationwide 1877 strike wave affected the couple profoundly. (The Illinois National Guard had been created in 1876 explicitly to protect the local ruling class from the workers they exploited and abused.) When Albert was blacklisted from his trade that same year—for a speech he had made—Lucy started a dressmaking business in their home to support the family, which now included two children—Albert Richard, Jr. (born 1879) and Lula Eda (born 1881)—whom they dreamed of raising as revolutionaries. Despite their many difficulties in "making a living" in hard times, Albert and Lucy were, by all accounts, very much in love and wildly happy together.

In Chicago in the 1870s, years before Haymarket, young Lucy became the Lucy Parsons we know: the selfless crusader for freedom, equality and solidarity—for workingclass self-emancipation from the terror and tyranny of Capital. Deeply moved by the plight of the poor and oppressed, and the workers' incessant struggle against exploitation and misery, she worked tirelessly throughout her life for the great Cause of social revolution—the cause of the underprivileged and downtrodden, the persecuted and impoverished, the homeless and incarcerated.

By 1879 Lucy was one of the main organizers and speakers for the Working Women's Union—a pioneer in unionizing women workers. In the early 1880s the Parsonses joined the Knights of Labor, and Lucy went out and organized the sewing women. Around 1883 they started to consider themselves anarchists. Both Albert and Lucy were addressing large workers' rallies on the Chicago lakefront and in meeting halls throughout the city. Their impact was far-reaching—Lucy's no less so than her husband's. Illustrating her ability to inspire working people to organize, a historian of the city's needle-trades unionism pointed out long ago that Lucy Parsons "influenced a large proportion of the Jewish workers of Chicago."[3]

That Lucy was a force to be reckoned with is beyond all doubt: The Chicago cops didn't call her "more dangerous than a thousand rioters" for nothing. A commanding presence, she was also a powerful speaker. In her youth as in her old age, people *loved* to hear Lucy Parsons speak; she had a musical voice, tremendous delivery, and no need of oratorical pretensions. As her friend Ben Reitman noted in later years, "she has the ability to tell her story simply and directly. In this she can move any audience."[4] In the matter of "anarchist outreach," Lucy had few if any equals.

One of the greatest agitators in U.S. history, Lucy Parsons was also a co-leader of important demonstrations; the November 1884 Thanksgiving Day protest and the April 1885 workers' march on the Board of Trade were especially notable. She also led a Christmas Day march to deliver Marshall Field his Christmas present: noisy demonstrators pelting his mansion with rotten tomatoes. Callous coward that he was, Field fled with his family to the North Shore. (Such flights by the wealthy elite were quite the rage then, just as "gated communities" are today.)

These massive manifestations of workingclass discontent were highly innovative actions—a kind of "street theater" that succeeded not only in scandalizing the bourgeoisie but above all in boosting the fighting morale of the working men and women who took part in them. Everyone who has written about Lucy Parsons has stressed her courage and audacity, but too few have recognized her creativity and imagination.

* * *

All through the 1870s/80s the Parsonses grew steadily more radical. Their dissatisfaction with the SLP's electoral focus and overall reformism had led them to anarchism, and in October 1883, with other like-minded fellow workers, they took part in organizing the International Working People's Association (IWPA). A year later—October '84—the first issue of the official English-language IWPA paper appeared in Chicago: the *Alarm*, a weekly that soon became one of the best-circulated and most-talked-about labor publications in the country. Edited by Albert, Lucy was a frequent contributor.

Indeed, it was her articles in the *Alarm*, more than anything else, that established her reputation as a firebrand—a dangerous and incendiary Red. Her 1884 address "To Tramps, the Unemployed, the Disinherited, and Miserable"—usually cited simply as

"To Tramps"—concludes by urging the poor to *"Learn the use of explosives!"* (Lucy's italics and exclamation-point). Reissued as a leaflet (reproduced in Ashbaugh's book), it became one of the most notorious documents in the history of U.S. anarchism.

Lucy Parsons's "To Tramps" was cited again and again, in the capitalist press, and by the prosecution in the Haymarket show-trial, to "prove" that Chicago's anarchists were the maddest of terrorists, seeking to foment civil war against a contented and peaceable public. The plain truth is that the city's ruling class, and its insanely out-of-control police force, were already terrorizing the working population well before "To Tramps" appeared in print. Explosives, and dynamite in particular, were still new and little known then, but military bigwigs (General Sheridan, for example), corporate executives and daily newspaper owners were urging their use against workers, and especially against workers on strike. As it happens, Lucy Parsons's reckless rhetoric in "To Tramps" is actually rather mild compared to the ferocious and cold-blooded anti-worker diatribes that regularly appeared in the capitalist dailies in those years. Here are just a few examples:

The President of the Pennsylvania Railroad, Tom Scott, recommended that strikers be given "the rifle diet." A *Chicago Times* editorial urged that "hand grenades should be thrown among those union sailors, who are striving to obtain higher wages and less hours. By such treatment they would be taught a valuable lesson, and other strikers could take warning from their fate." And according to the *New York Herald*, "the best meal that can be given a ragged tramp is a leaden one, and it should be supplied in sufficient quantities to satisfy the most voracious appetite." The *Chicago Tribune* had notions of its own: "When a tramp asks you for bread, put strychnine or arsenic on it and he will not trouble you any more, and others will keep out of the neighborhood."

Were any of these ruling-class advocates of mass murder ever arrested, called into court, tried by a jury, convicted for their crimes? Of course not, for it is they who *own* the police and the courts.

"To Tramps" attained notoriety overnight, and retained it; it is undoubtedly one of Lucy's most-quoted tracts. Her writings on the crime of lynching, however, and on other racist violence, are

7

hardly ever mentioned, despite the fact that they were, as Robin Kelley has emphasized, "published several years before Ida B. Wells's famous pronouncements on the subject."[5] In these anti-racist writings, Lucy—who in her youth had experienced KKK terror first-hand—advocated armed self-defense. In other words, some seventy-five years before the advent of Robert F. Williams, Malcolm X, Max Stanford, the Revolutionary Action Movement and the Black Panther Party, Lucy Parsons upheld the principle that the oppressed had the right and the duty to defend themselves by any means necessary.

The IWPA was basically an anarchist organization, but its anarchism had a lot of Marxism mixed into it. Many anarchists of that time and place—including Albert and Lucy Parsons—considered Karl Marx an anarchist.

Lucy's later writings tend to be less inflammatory than some of her texts in the *Alarm*, but she remained a direct-actionist her whole life. "We 'endorse' nothing," she wrote, "but take the chances for everything in attempting to abolish the wage system."

It was not the Chicago anarchists' advocacy of self-defense (or of "propaganda by the deed") that the owners of industry found frightening; for the employing class, *that* was just a smokescreen to hoodwink a gullible public. What really scared the bosses (*a.k.a.* robber barons) was the anarchists' effective support and leadership of the workers' struggle for the eight-hour working day and higher wages. For the ruling class, a threat to their precious power and profits is the horror of horrors, and the only unforgivable crime.

Thus Chicago's ruling elite—manufacturers, newspaper owners, railroad magnates, businessmen, cops, the clergy, a sizeable number of professional criminals (thoroughly "respectable," of course), and other "pillars of the community"— resolved to crush the flourishing and steadily growing anarchist movement, and by doing so, to disorganize organized labor and reduce the working class to passivity.

* * *

The May 1886 Haymarket events, and their various sequels, have provoked an extensive literature.[6] Several of Lucy's articles

8

in this book discuss those events in depth, and others focus on specific details. A short outline should suffice here.

On the First of May 1886, a beautiful, sunny Saturday, Albert and Lucy Parsons led an enthusiastic parade of 80,000 working men, women and children down Chicago's Michigan Avenue, inaugurating a general strike for the eight-hour day. The eight-hour struggle was intended to be nationwide in scope, but Chicago proved to be the major battleground. Many factory-owners and other businessmen agreed to the strikers' demands, and a resounding workers' victory appeared to be in sight.

Anti-union forces, however, were up to their dirty work, as usual. On May 3, at the McCormick Reaper (later International Harvester) plant on the South Side, a contingent of cops led by the sinister Capt. John "Blackjack" Bonfield attacked an unarmed group of strikers, shooting several and killing at least two of them. A bloodthirsty and crooked cop—later removed from the force for theft, taking bribes, and other offenses—Bonfield had long specialized in anti-worker violence (breaking up meetings, beating up street-speakers, etc.), and union-busting in general.

On the evening of May 4, some 3000 workers gathered at Haymarket Square on Randolph Street to protest the preceding day's police shooting. A little after ten o'clock, as the meeting was about to close—it had started to rain, and most of the crowd had left, including Albert and Lucy Parsons and their two children—Bonfield suddenly marched in with 180 heavily armed cops. Someone—nobody knows who, but Lucy, Albert and many others were sure it was an *agent provocateur*—threw a bomb. In the ensuing police riot, seven cops and numerous workers were killed, and many more workers were wounded—shot by the cops' crossfire. (There is no evidence that any of the workers were armed.)

The rest is history at its bleakest: the city's first big Red Scare; massive arrests of anarchists, socialists, trade-unionists, and innocent bystanders; midnight raids on workers' homes; newspaper hysteria; police suppression of the labor press; and a ludicrous frame-up trial of eight of Chicago's outstanding labor leaders, all of whom happened to be anarchists. Although there was no evidence against any of them—even the prosecution admitted that the defendants had nothing to do with the bomb-throwing—a packed

9

jury quickly found them guilty. Four—George Engel, Albert Fischer, Albert Parsons, and Louis Lingg—were sentenced to death. The first three were hanged; Lingg was murdered in his cell, or committed suicide; and three others—Samuel Fielden, Oscar Neebe, and Michael Schwab—were sent to prison. Not one was guilty of anything more than free speech and union-organizing.

Needless to say, the Red Scare also brought the collapse, for several years, of the eight-hour struggle.

Criminalizing the working class, and especially the poorest and most radical among them, has always—long before Haymarket, and right down to our own day—been a component of the capitalist injustice system.

Lucy Parsons's response to the ordeal of her husband and the other Haymarket comrades was, characteristically, to *take action*. She immediately helped organize an extensive Haymarket defense campaign. She wrote articles for workers' papers around the country and abroad, as well as numerous letters to comrades and well-known public figures, requesting their aid. On a speaking tour that took her to seventeen states, she not only introduced large audiences to the truth about the Haymarket events, and thereby helped change public opinion on the case, but also raised funds for further defense activity and for an appeal.

Characteristically, too, her writings and speeches in defense of her husband and his fellow imprisoned anarchists focused on capitalism's injustice to the whole working class.

On many occasions police broke up Lucy Parsons's public meetings and threw her in jail. Decades later, "Chicago's Finest" —and their equivalents in other cities—were still in the habit of denying her Constitutional rights, shutting down her talks, and carting her off to jail. Her arrest-record must have been staggering. During a free-speech fight out West in the 1910s she said, "Every jail on the Pacific Coast knows me."

Hounded by police, thrown into jail, and reviled in the capitalist press, she nonetheless persisted and did in fact win over a good portion of the public to the side of truth and justice.

Six years after the monstrous "trial," Illinois Governor John P. Altgeld unconditionally pardoned the three remaining Haymarket anarchist prisoners—Fielden, Schwab and Neebe—at the cost of his political career.[7] Fully vindicating all that Lucy Parsons had been arguing since the 1887 trial, Altgeld's 1893 *Reasons for Pardoning* message—a classic document in the struggle for freedom in the U.S.—highlighted the obvious innocence of all the Haymarket martyrs and unsparingly condemned the preposterously unfair trial, the openly prejudiced jury, the deceitful prosecutor and above all the bigoted judge and his "malicious ferocity."

Like most anarchists of her generation, Lucy respected Altgeld more than any other elected official in U.S. history. In the preface to her 1915 edition of *Reasons for Pardoning*, she praised him as "one of those rare characters who could remain true to his high ideals in spite of politics." Her tribute naturally focused on his pardoning of the anarchists, but she also emphasized that, at the time of his death, Altgeld was actively engaged in defending the rights of the oppressed people of South Africa.

* * *

A central figure in the Haymarket events and the long-drawn-out defense campaign, Lucy Parsons continued to spread the word about Haymarket in later years, especially to the younger generation of labor radicals. To the end of her days she was active in the two Haymarket-derived holidays—May Day and November 11—and she spoke on the subject at countless venues over the years.

Her book, *The Life of Albert R. Parsons*—a collection of Albert's letters, articles, and speeches, first published in 1889 and reissued twice—has been a major source for all subsequent writing on "Chicago Idea" anarchism and the Haymarket tragedy. Another of her compilations, *The Famous Speeches of the Chicago Anarchists* went through many printings of thousands of copies each. At least up to World War Two, these books were in every union hall and radical library in the country, and in many other countries as well.

Lucy sold these and other revolutionary publications on her speaking tours, at union meetings, strike rallies, anarchist and IWW picnics, at Bughouse Square—Chicago's celebrated free-speech park, across from The Newberry Library—and on the street (she was a familiar sight in downtown Chicago for years).

11

It would be hard to exaggerate her influence on the younger generation of radicals—and that influence was not confined to the U.S. In his history of British anarchism, John Quail commented on the impact of her 1888 tour of England and Scotland, as the guest of the Socialist League:

> She came and made a strong impression both at her London meetings and on her provincial tour which was also arranged by the League. She was no pathetic, sorrow-struck victim. She came as a propagandist to whom tragedy had given a stronger voice. Her visit, more than any other factor, accelerated the drift towards a "definitely Anarchist attitude" in the Socialist League.[8]

More recently, in connection with that same British speaking tour, Paul Gilroy in his book *The Black Atlantic* has raised the question of how Lucy Parsons's "encounters with William Morris, Annie Besant, and Peter Kropotkin [might] impact upon a rewriting of the history of English radicalism."[9]

Years later, in 1909, as an agitator for the Industrial Workers of the World—as historian Mark Leier has pointed out—Lucy Parsons's speaking tour of British Columbia during a free-speech fight "provided a rallying point for the Vancouver activists" and helped the IWWs and other radicals win a clear-cut victory.[10]

For her, the revolutionary future was alive in the direct actions, slowdowns, strikes and solidarity of the present. A fearless fighter on the front lines of the class war, she was always ready for the next struggle.

Alas, too many summaries of Lucy Parsons's life continue to focus on Haymarket and her husband's judicial murder to the exclusion of all else. In truth, her writings and speeches on the events of 1886-87, however important, are a relatively small part of her life's work. Several of her articles relate the injustice of the Haymarket trial to later frame-ups, such as that of "Big Bill" Haywood, Charles Moyer and George Petitbone in 1906, and of Tom Mooney and the Gastonia Strikers in later years. Her point was not to memorialize the past but to show historic continuity, and above all to advance the cause of workingclass emancipation here and now.

In the fragmentary records about Lucy Parsons, much is uncertain, but one thing that is beyond doubt is her passionate sincerity and devotion to world transformation: "building a new society in the shell of the old." Practically every line she wrote was meant to awaken readers to the urgent need to abolish wage-slavery and the repressive state that supports it.

* * *

Keep in mind that Lucy Parsons was active in the cause ten years before Haymarket, and stayed active—an indefatigable militant—for fifty-five years after the miserable trial. That's six and a half decades "in the service of the revolution."

And all through the years, the causes she defended were remarkably consistent: anarchism, revolutionary socialism, the IWW's revolutionary industrial unionism, and such related causes as racial and sexual equality, struggles of the unemployed, anti-imperialism, freedom of speech and assembly, real separation of church and state, birth control, abolition of child labor, and—by no means least—immediate release of all class-war prisoners (that is, activists imprisoned for union-organizing or for radical activities).

As an activist/supporter of these many causes which for her were really one great cause, Lucy Parsons recognized that only a well-organized mass workingclass movement could realize the revolutionary dream of a free society. With that in mind, she co-founded, joined, and worked with many diverse organizations over the years. Between the mid-1870s and the turn of the century she had taken part in the Greenback Labor Party, the Socialistic Labor Party, the Knights of Labor, the Secular Union, the International Working People's Association, the Working Women's Union, and the Social Democracy. In the new century she identified herself, at various times, with several anarchist groups, the Socialist Party, the Industrial Workers of the World (IWW), the Syndicalist League of North America (SLNA), International Labor Defense (ILD), and a number of open forums, including the hobohemian Dil Pickle Club.

Some of Lucy's more narrow-minded critics considered her willingness to work with such different groups flighty or opportunistic. In Lucy's view, however, the *movement* of the working *class* was much more important than any particular organization. She believed in promoting workingclass emancipation in every way she could. Today, many would call her involvement in the

13

activities of various groups a form of networking, solidarity and mutual aid.

Lucy's involvement in several different anarchist groups, and in their factional disputes, is lightly sketched in Ashbaugh's biography. Very little of the inner life of these groups is known to us, but clearly Lucy Parsons was a strong presence in every group she took part in. We know that she was adamant in her support for revolutionary and workingclass anarchism, and critical—even disdainful—of the middle-class currents that eventually came to dominate U.S. anarchism. A prolific contributor to an impressive number of anarchist periodicals, she spoke to anarchist groups, and/or to large public meetings organized by anarchists, from coast to coast in the U.S. as well as in England and Canada. She knew and worked with—at one time or another—many of the most prominent anarchists of the day, including Peter Kropotkin, Errico Malatesta, Johann Most, C. L. James, Jo Labadie, Voltairine de Cleyre, Emma Goldman, Ben Reitman, and later such younger militants as Irving Abrams, Boris Yelensky and Sam Dolgoff.

Lucy Parsons was, unquestionably, a major figure in anarchism, not only in the U.S., but internationally.

Her association with Eugene V. Debs's Social Democracy, and its successor, the Socialist Party, was brief, but like many anarchists and IWWs, she was steadfast in her admiration for Debs himself. Like Debs, Lucy was close to the far left Charles H. Kerr Company, whose *International Socialist Review* enthusiastically promoted her *Life of Albert R. Parsons* ("tells the facts . . . in as full and accurate a manner as they are to be found anywhere [and shows] that the present ruling class will stop at nothing in their endeavor to terrorize those who threaten their rulership"). Later, under Mary Marcy's editorship, the *Review* featured many display ads for the *Famous Speeches.*

Of the post-Haymarket groups that attracted her, the Industrial Workers of the World loomed largest in her life. As a delegate to its founding (1905) convention, she made what many regard as that convention's most outstanding speech. She boldly proclaimed American labor's total solidarity with the working men and women of the entire world, and specifically included the workers of China and Africa; at that time most American Federation of Labor (AFL) unions upheld a white-male-only policy. She was there, she said, representing the poorest of the poor, the most oppressed and defenseless sectors of the producing class. She urged a special effort to organize women, and even put in a good word for prostitutes ("my sisters whom I can see in the night when I go out in Chicago"). To top it all off, Delegate Parsons foresaw the sit-down as the strike of the future.

After the convention, she edited a pro-IWW newspaper, *The Liberator*—taking the name from William Lloyd Garrison's famous pre-Civil-War paper, and thus linking the IWW's cause of abolishing wage-slavery with the earlier Abolitionist movement. She also went on an extensive speaking tour for the new union.

Although her activity in the IWW was sporadic, Lucy Parsons remained close to the union for the rest of her life. She was a frequent and popular speaker in IWW halls all over the country, and included many Wobblies—as IWW members began to be called around 1913—among her friends. In the IWW, more than any other organization, she saw the fulfilment of the "Chicago Idea" anarchism that she and Albert helped develop in the 1880s.

Interestingly, Lucy's companion during the last four decades of her life, George Markstall, was a longtime Wobbly who kept his dues paid up till the day he died.

Very little is known about Lucy's involvement in William Z. Foster's short-lived Syndicalist League (1912-14), whose mailing address (1000 South Paulina) also happened to be hers. A small split-off from the IWW, the SLNA criticized the IWW's "dual unionism" and called for "boring from within" the existing AFL unions. Lucy Parsons, one of the least sectarian characters in the history of U.S. radicalism, probably thought the workers' movement was big enough to include both currents.

Critical though she was of the AFL bureaucrats' conservative policies, she did not want to ignore its million-plus rank and file, and in fact her cross-country tours often involved speaking engagements under craft-union auspices. Widely respected throughout the ranks of organized labor as a veteran of the eight-hour struggle, she was able to introduce radical ideas to audiences that might well have been put off by a blatantly anti-AFL speaker. According to Elizabeth Gurley Flynn, it was Lucy Parsons, more than anyone else, who "accustomed trade union men to listen respectfully to a woman speaking for Labor."[11]

In any event, Lucy Parsons had many comrades, friends and admirers in AFL unions, particularly in the Chicago Federation of Labor, and above all among the printers. Widely recognized as the most democratic of all unions, the International Typographical Union differed in many important respects from other AFL affiliates. Early on, for example, the ITU had welcomed women as well as people of color into its ranks, and its membership included an impressive number of distinguished radicals, social critics, and labor editors, such as Abolitionist Martin F. Conway, Mark Twain, Henry George, Jo Labadie, Alzina P. Stevens, Emma Langdon, and Otto Huiswood. For fourteen years prior to his judicial murder, Albert Parsons was an active and well-liked member of Chicago Typographical Union No. 16, which played a major role in the eight-hour struggle in the 1880s and later. Although Lucy briefly (1905-06) used the IWW label on her printed matter instead of the Allied Printing Trades (AFL) label, she still remained close to many union printers and friendly toward the local itself.

When Henry P. Rosemont, a young San Francisco printer, moved to Chicago in 1926, he met several old-timers in No. 16 —among them the Gritzmacher brothers and Canadian-born printer-poet Alexander Spencer—who had known Albert and Lucy Parsons "back when," and who had stayed in touch with Lucy through the years.[12] Younger Chicago printer-radicals—most notably Carl Berreitter, George Koop, Sam Ball, Donald Crocker and "Red Martha" Biegler—also knew Lucy well.

No. 16 was not a "radical" union, but even its more conservative officers were always friendly to Lucy Parsons, who was, after all, a labor movement legend and a living reminder of heroic struggles. Henry Rosemont recalled one of her visits to the union's headquarters in 1941 or 42, a few months before she died. She was in her late eighties, ailing and infirm, and had come to apply to the union for relief. The printers welcomed her warmly, and all who were present—each and every one of No. 16's officers and members of the Executive Committee—gave Lucy Parsons a full day's pay.

Several of the union printers just mentioned—Berreitter, Ball, Biegler, Crocker—were active in Chicago's Dil Pickle Club ("the indoor Bughouse Square") and other open forums, as was Lucy Parsons herself.[13] Indeed, she appears to have been one of the most assiduous forum-goers of all time. As speaker, panelist, moderator, or questioner from the floor, she lost few opportunities to exercise her right to free speech, and thus to give people something to think about.

At the Dil Pickle, whose founders were mostly Wobbly soap-boxers, past and present, and whose habitués included radicals and "characters" of all kinds, Lucy Parsons spoke at several Haymarket Memorials in the 1920s and 30s, at least once with a slide show. Her long association with the Dil Pickle is significant; many older radicals of the time, as well as "hard-line" dogmatists of the Communist Party type, frowned on the club's emphasis on playfulness and poetry, and its overall bohemianism, but such "deviations" evidently did not trouble Lucy Parsons. Her openness to new and different ways of being radical, and her willingness to learn from young people are among her most engaging qualities.

Far more than most labor radicals of her time, she tried to keep up with everything vibrant, daring, rebellious, and alive. If she were around today I'm sure she would drop in at the meetings of the Chicago Surrealist Group, and regularly check out such places as Heartland Café, the Velvet Lounge, and the Hothouse just to see what's happening.

In the old-time forum-circuit, Lucy Parsons was especially active in the Chicago Society of Anthropology Forum. According to Sophia Fagin's 1939 University of Chicago Master's Thesis, *Public Forums in Chicago*, the group was founded in 1895, just after the World's Fair, by supporters of Ida B. Wells's protest against the exclusion of African Americans from the World's Congress of Religions. Emphatically anti-racist from the start, the group declared that the purpose of the new Society was

> to provide a forum in which tolerance and liberality are encouraged and a welcome hand extended to everyone without regard to race, creed, or color; giving all views, however widely divergent, a respectful hearing.

17

During its almost forty years of continuous activity, its roster of speakers featured a broad spectrum of authors, radicals, scholars, and activists, including Ida B. Wells, Thomas J. Morgan, Lillian Herstein, Curtis Reese, Ben Reitman, and Slim Brundage.

Lucy Parsons's participation in the Anthropology Society Forum reveals that her range of interests was considerably greater than has often been assumed by her critics. In the years 1920-22, as indicated in the *Chicago Daily News* listings of "Meetings and Lectures," she lectured or debated at the Society on such topics as marriage, rent extortion, Mexico, Catholicism, the labor movement, Russia, juvenile delinquency, and the French Revolution.

Her probable acquaintance with Ida B. Wells through the Anthropological Society makes us wonder about Lucy's other relations with African Americans. Historian Barbara Bair is surely on the mark when she writes that Lucy Parsons's "kind of activism set an example for black people's involvement in various movements of the American left," but little information is available.[14] The IWW had many black members, including several who lived in Chicago: Did Lucy know any of them? She could easily have met young black radicals as well as well-known figures such as Jack Johnson at the Dil Pickle, but no record of such meetings has turned up. In 1932, Lucy—together with Tom Mooney's mother and Viola Montgomery, mother of one of the Scottsboro defendants—placed a wreath on the Haymarket monument at Waldheim (now Forest Home) cemetery.[15] And black Communist Ishmael Flory has recalled how thrilled he was, as a youngster in the movement, when he saw Lucy Parsons for the first time in a Chicago May Day parade in the mid-1930s.

These examples are few in number and meager in detail, but stimulating nonetheless. Here is a wide field for research! Further digging into the history of the Anthropology Society, and other inter-racial forums, would be a good way to begin.

In the *Daily News* announcement of one of her Anthropology Society talks, on "Mexico and Mexicans," Lucy was described as "a native." Another announcement referred to her as a "descendant from Aztecs." Chicago old-timers recalled that Albert Parsons usually described his wife as a "Spanish Aztec lady." Are such descriptions affirmations of her "Mexicanism" or denials of her

18

blackness? We really don't know, do we? She did defend and raise funds for the Mexican Revolution of 1910. But beyond that, all we know is that we know even less about her association with Mexicans and Native Americans than we do about her association with African Americans.

If the Anthropology Society and the Dil Pickle were Lucy's favorite forums, she also appeared at many more: the anarchist Free Society Forum, the IWW Forum, the Proletarian Party Forum, Ben Reitman's Hobo College—and no doubt others that are not so well-remembered. We know, for example, that at least once she spoke at Martha Biegler's explicitly socialist-feminist Woman's Forum. As announced in the April 5, 1919 issue of the Chicago Federation of Labor paper, *The New Majority*, Lucy Parsons joined Biegler, Mabel Kanka and Edna Fine in a panel discussion on the theme that "the majority of men are low-grade morons."

When we consider that she also frequently addressed union meetings and strike rallies, that she participated in the discussions at the Radical Bookshop, and that she was for many years—as Studs Terkel has often recalled—a "regular" at Bughouse Square, it becomes clear that Lucy Parsons was one of the most renowned and persistent public speakers in Windy City history.

From the mid-1920s through much of the 30s Lucy Parsons was active in the International Labor Defense (ILD), a Communist Party offshoot (or "front group"), specifically devoted to publicizing, defending, and freeing class-war prisoners. Especially in its early years, under the direction of Lucy's friend, former Wobbly James P. Cannon, the ILD was a broad-based and non-sectarian defense group; socialist Eugene Debs, feminist Alice Stone Blackwell, anarchist Carlo Tresca, Ralph Chaplin and several other Wobblies also took part in it. At a time when anarchism in the U.S. had reached low ebb, and the IWW had also fallen on hard times, the ILD's defense work appeared to many militants as a worthwhile practical activity. And so it came to pass that Lucy Parsons, who had spearheaded the defense agitation for the Haymarket anarchists of the 1880s, spent a good part of her last years agitating for the defense of the IWW's Centralia prisoners, Tom Mooney, Warren Billings, Sacco and Vanzetti, Angelo Herndon, and the Scottsboro defendants.

It was doubtless her activity in the ILD that led some people to believe that she actually joined the Communist Party, though she explicitly denied this in letters to old friends. The careless and unfounded assertion in Ashbaugh's biography—that Lucy joined the CP—has since been repeated *ad nauseam* by other writers, and by Ashbaugh herself in the *Encyclopedia of the American Left.* Thus the unlikely image of Lucy Parsons as Communist—or worse, as The Anarchist Who Became a Communist—added more confusion to the already confused mythology of the U.S. Left.

Throughout the period in which Lucy worked in the ILD, she also frequented such very different groups as the Dil Pickle, the IWW, the anarchist Free Society Group, and even the Proletarian Party, all of which were detested by the CP. Had Lucy Parsons, a veteran radical of great stature, actually signed up in the CP the Party apparatus would have boasted about it in banner headlines and special features. But nothing of the sort happened. When she died in 1942, her obituary in the CP's *Daily Worker*—by Elizabeth Gurley Flynn—made no mention of Party membership. Flynn's later autobiographical writings are also silent on the matter—as are the autobiographies of William Z. Foster and longtime Chicago Communists Harry Haywood and Claude Lightfoot (the latter two, in fact, do not mention Lucy Parsons at all).

It is especially bizarre to think that Lucy Parsons would have joined the CP in the late 1930s, when the Party had swung so far to the right that its main slogan was "Communism is Twentieth-Century Americanism," and its public meetings often involved singing "The Star-Spangled Banner." Lucy Parsons was too much of a revolutionary for the so-called "Popular Front": the Communists' proposed "alliance" of labor and liberal bourgeoisie, a Stalinist version of that old chestnut, the "harmony between Capital and Labor." As she wrote in mid-decade to an old anarchist comrade: "The Roosevelt wind has blown the radical movement to hell!"[16]

Although she was disappointed by the weak and disorganized character of U.S. anarchism from the 1920s on, and deplored its non-involvement in workers' struggles, Lucy Parsons never renounced anarchism itself. To the end she upheld the libertarian socialist ideals that motivated the 1880s IWPA as well as the "One Big Union" of the twentieth-century IWW.

* * *

Lucy Parsons's last few years were marred by the ravages of old age, illness and loneliness. Her closest friends were long gone—deceased or living far away. Physically debilitated and nearly blind, she was unable to take the long walks that had been such a pleasant part of her daily life for so many years. Eyesight problems also deprived her of another of her greatest pleasures: *reading.* (Lucy's library included much of the world's great literature, including the complete works of Victor Hugo, and many volumes of poetry.)

She did enjoy visits from old Wobblies—and young ones too, such as Art Weinberg[17] of the Chicago Junior Wobbly Union—as well as from individual anarchists, socialists, Communists, and other friends. She also did her best to keep active in labor's cause. She was the featured speaker at the huge 1937 Fiftieth Anniversary November 11 Haymarket Memorial organized by the Free Society Group and held at the Amalgamated Clothing Workers' Union hall at 333 North Ashland. Anarchist/Wobbly Sam Dolgoff, who also spoke on that occasion, recalled that Lucy was "bent with age" but "still defiant, still hurling curses at the powers-that-be, still calling for the overthrow of capitalism."[18]

In one of her last public speeches (February 23, 1941) she addressed members of the Farm Equipment Workers on strike at International Harvester—successor to the old McCormick Reaper Works where, in May 1886, police violence had provoked the famous protest meeting at Haymarket Square. A couple months later she was the guest of honor on the Farm Equipment Workers' float in the 1941 May Day Parade—her last May Day.

Lucy Parsons died on March 7, 1942—at the age of eighty-nine. The wood stove at her house at 3130 North Troy had caught fire. Virtually blind by then, she got trapped in the fire and died. Her companion, George Markstall—himself quite elderly and far from tip-top condition—tried to save her, but suffered serious burns and other injuries in the attempt, and died the next day.

Some three hundred people attended the Lucy Parsons/George Markstall funeral, and dedicated the Lucy Parsons marker at Waldheim, a few feet away from the Haymarket monument. The speakers included her old friend Ben Reitman, and J. O. Benthal of the

Communist Party. Win Stracke, who later founded the Old Town School of Folk Music, sang "I Dreamed I Saw Joe Hill Last Night."

* * *

The reawakening of interest in Lucy Parsons seems to have started in Chicago in the mid-1960s at Solidarity Bookshop—an IWW/anarchist/surrealist bookstore that has been variously described as the last stand of the "Left Wing of the Beat Generation" and the first glimmer of the "dropout culture." It was located in the then-very-rundown Lincoln Park area, a few blocks from the old Wobbly hall at Halsted and Fullerton.

When the young Wobblies who opened Solidarity learned that Lucy and Albert Parsons and other Haymarket anarchists had lived in that very neighborhood some eighty-odd years earlier, they began to research the subject. Henry David's *History of the Haymarket Affair* provided the basic facts; Captain Schaack's *Anarchy and Anarchists* offered wonderful engravings; and Lucy Parsons's *Famous Speeches* (a nearby used bookstore happened to have several copies on hand) gave them a strong sense of what "Chicago Idea" anarchism was all about.

Solidarity Bookshop's beautiful series of "Anarchist/Revolutionary Calendars," designed and calligraphed by Tor Faegre, drew heavily on Haymarket and its imagery, as did the group's various mimeographed publications—most notably their "wild-eyed, incendiary" journal, *The Rebel Worker*. At some point (*circa* 1967-69) they printed a 17" x 22" poster of Lucy Parsons. The long-awaited Lucy Parsons revival was on!

Carolyn Ashbaugh's biography (1976), Paul Avrich's *The Haymarket Tragedy* (1984), and the *Haymarket Scrapbook*, edited by Dave Roediger and Franklin Rosemont (1986) were other landmarks in the steadily expanding rediscovery of Lucy Parsons. Ashbaugh's book—which sold equally well to labor unions, feminist collectives, and scattered outposts of the Old and New Left—inspired a large number of articles on Lucy, as well as Lucy Parsons t-shirts, postcards, and other ephemera. The *Haymarket Scrapbook* also did much to keep Lucy in the public eye; its 250-plus images (including several of Lucy) have turned up in countless "underground" and "alternative" publications.

In 1986 (the Haymarket Centennial), actress Alma Washington began doing her wonderful performances of Lucy Parsons as soapboxer, and she has kept on doing them—in infinite variety —ever since: at schools, union meetings, strike rallies, and demonstrations. In recent years, in connection with The Newberry Library's annual book sale, Alma has also performed at Bughouse Square, where labor songster Allen Schwartz often sings his lovely "Lucy Parsons" song.

Movement artists who have portrayed Lucy Parsons include Carlos Cortez, Susan Greene, Mike Alewitz, Marjorie Woodruff, and no doubt many others. Cortez's linocut poster has gone through several printings, and is now also available as a Charles H. Kerr postcard. Greene included Lucy in a mural at the Bound Together Anarchist Bookstore in San Francisco. Two Alewitz murals also feature Lucy: one in Mexico City and another in the Chicago Teamsters' building. Woodruff's memorial to Lucy in Chicago's Wicker Park features an "uncomfortable bench for uncomfortable thoughts."

Since the Lucy Parsons revival started in a bookshop, it is fitting that another bookstore in the Solidarity tradition is doing a good job of seeing to it that Lucy Parsons's revolutionary legacy lives today. The Lucy Parsons Center in Cambridge, Massachusetts, happens to be one of the best movement bookstores in the country (among much else, it stocks the complete line of Charles H. Kerr books).

And don't forget to check out the Lucy Parsons Project website: www.lucyparsonsproject.org

* * *

But some people will ask: Are the writings and speeches of Lucy Parsons merely of "historic" interest? Aren't they "dated," written as they were in times so very different from our own?

To my view, the up-to-the-minute relevance of these powerful texts—their *vital meaning today*—vastly outweighs their historic interest, great as that is. Although written long ago, these texts tackle the major problems of *our* time.

Furthermore, I emphatically reject the conventional supposition that the sources of human misery and despair have really changed that much from Lucy Parsons's day to our own. Those who cause our miseries and despairs (the ruling class) would of course like us to think so, and by misdirection and hype they have managed to mix up the signs and symptoms so that some things today are (or seem) a little better now than in Lucy's day, while others are in fact much worse.

To such deception, Lucy Parsons's illuminating and eye-opening clarity is the perfect antidote. Everything she says about the capitalist system and its repressive state is still very much to the point. Here and there her terminology may be a bit old-fashioned, but her critique of *essentials*—exploitation, misery, wage-slavery, police brutality, the frame-up system, state terror, homelessness, the lying media, and all the rest of the rottenness known as capitalism—is on the button, as fresh as the latest news-flash but infinitely more truthful.

Try to imagine the world as it would be today had Lucy Parsons's vision prevailed: a world without wage-slavery, racism, poverty, prisons, ecocide, wars, and other miserabilist horrors.

Her writings are among the best and strongest in the history of U.S. anarchism. Some of her argumentation was freely drawn from Marx or Kropotkin, or from other anarchists and poets, but the most daring ideas are hers, and she expresses them with an ardor and intensity that must have kept her listeners on the edge of their seats. A deeply *moving* speaker, with her beautiful, melodious voice, she moved the hearts and minds of the oppressed to organize and to overthrow the oppressor.

Oppression was something she knew a lot about. Her long and often traumatic experience of the capitalist injustice system—from KKK terror in her youth, through Haymarket and the judicial murder of her husband, to the U.S. government's war on the IWW —made her not "just another victim" but an extraordinarily articulate *witness* to, and vehement crusader against, *all* injustice. That kind of direct experience gave her a credibility, and an *actuality,* that those who lack such experience just don't have. And that credibility and actuality continue to resound in her writings.

Resounding, too, is her impassioned insistence that there is only one way out of the capitalist prison: the way of *social revolution.* It was the way Lucy Parsons urged all of her adult life: the collective creation, by the workers of the world, of a new society in which complete liberty for all is assured by making human rights triumph over property rights.

Lucy Parsons's life and writings reflect her true-to-the-bone heroism. She was fearless in the face of authority, and her rebellious spirit lives on in her forceful, liberating words. Her language sparkles with the love of freedom and the passion of revolt. She embodied the marvelous watchword of poet Jayne Cortez: "Find your own voice and use it/Use your own voice and find it."[19]

The working class of her times was lucky to have such a light, and we are lucky to have these writings.

Chicago, November 2003

NOTES

1. Robin D. G. Kelley, *Freedom Dreams: The Black Radical Imagination.* Boston: Beacon Press, 2003, 41-42.

2. William J. Adelman, *Haymarket Revisited: A Tour Guide of Labor History and Ethnic Neighborhoods Connected with the Haymarket Affair.* Chicago: The Illinois Labor History Society, Second Edition, 1986.

3. Wilfred Carsel, *A History of the Chicago Ladies Garment Workers' Union.* Chicago: Normandie House, 1946, 23.

4. Ben Reitman, *Following the Monkey,* unpublished autobiography in the Reitman Papers, Special Collections, Library of the University of Illinois at Chicago, 306.

5. Robin D. G. Kelley, "Lucy Parsons," in Darlene Clark Hine, ed., *Black Women in America: An Historical Encyclopedia.* Brooklyn: Carlson, 1993, 910.

6. See especially Paul Avrich, *The Haymarket Tragedy.* Princeton: Princeton University Press, 1984; Dave Roediger and Franklin Rosemont, eds., *Haymarket Scrapbbook.* Chicago: Charles H. Kerr, 1986; and Robert W. Glenn, *The Haymarket Affair: An Annotated Bibliography.* Westport, CT: Greenwood Press, 1993.

7. John Peter Altgeld, *Reasons for Pardoning the Haymarket Anarchists,* with an Introduction by Leon M. Despres and an Afterword by Clarence Darrow. Chicago: Charles H. Kerr, 1986.

8. John Quail, *The Slow-Burning Fuse: The Lost History of the British Anarchists.* London: Granada, 1978, 82.

9. Paul Gilroy, *The Black Atlantic: Modernity and Double Consciousness.* Cambridge, MA: Harvard University Press, 18.

10. Mark Leier, *Where the Fraser River Flows: The Industrial Workers of the World in British Columbia.* Vancouver: New Star Books, 1990, 67.

11. Elizabeth Gurley Flynn, "Lucy Parsons: Tribute to a Heroine of Labor," *Daily Worker,* March 11, 1942, 4.

12. Henry P. Rosemont, "Albert Parsons, Union Printer," in *Haymarket Scrapbook, op. cit.,* 36-37.

13. Franklin Rosemont, *The Rise & Fall of the Dil Pickle: Jazz-Age Chicago's Wildest & Most Outrageously Creative Nightspot.* Chicago: Charles H. Kerr, 2003.

14. Barbara Bair, "Though Justice Sleeps," in Robin D. G. Kelley and Earl Lewis, eds., *To Make Our World Anew: A History of African Americans.* New York: Oxford University Press, 2000, 342-343.

15. Curt Gentry, *Frame-Up: The Incredible Case of Tom Mooney and Warren K. Billings.* New York: W, W. Norton, 1967, 366.

16. Letter to Carl Nold, January 31, 1934; copy in the Carolyn Ashbaugh files in the Charles H. Kerr Publishing Company Archives, Special Collections, The Newberry Library, Chicago.

17. Art Weinberg (who called himself "Art Hopkins" in his IWW days) went on to become a leading biographer/anthologist of Clarence Darrow.

18. Sam Dolgoff, "Recollections of Lucy Parsons & the Fiftieth Anniversary of November 11," in *Haymarket Scrapbook, op cit.*, 246.

19. Jayne Cortez, *Somewhere in Advance of Nowhere.* New York: High Risk Books, 1996, 116.

Lucy Parsons, 1889, National Portrait Gallery, Smithsonian Institution

LUCY PARSONS

FREEDOM, EQUALITY & SOLIDARITY

Writings & Speeches, 1878-1937

Speaking at an anarchist picnic, 1880s

*The disinherited
must work out their own salvation
in their own way.*
—**Lucy Parsons**—

On a Speaking Tour in England and Scotland
(From the magazine *Commonweal*,
London, November 10, 1888)

THE PRINCIPLES OF ANARCHISM

Comrades and Friends: I think I cannot open my address more appropriately than by stating my experience in my long connection with the reform movement.

It was during the great railroad strike of 1877 that I first became interested in what is known as the "Labor Question." I then thought as many thousands of earnest, sincere people think, that the aggregate power operating in human society, known as government, could be made an instrument in the hands of the oppressed to alleviate their sufferings. But a closer study of the origin, history and tendency of governments convinced me that this was a mistake.

I came to understand how organized governments used their concentrated power to retard progress by their ever-ready means of silencing the voice of discontent if raised in vigorous protest against the machinations of the scheming few, who always did, always will and always must rule in the councils of nations where majority rule is recognized as the only means of adjusting the affairs of the people.

I came to understand that such concentrated power can be always wielded in the interest of the few and at the expense of the many. Government in its last analysis is this power reduced to a science. Governments never lead; they follow progress. When the prison, stake or scaffold can no longer silence the voice of the protesting minority, progress moves on a step, but not until then.

I will state this contention in another way: I learned by close study that it made no difference what fair promises a political party, out of power, might make to the people in order to secure their confidence, when once securely established in control of the affairs of society; that they were after all but human, with all the human attributes of the politician. Among these are: First, to remain in power at all hazards; if not individually, then those holding essentially the same views as the administration must be kept in control. Second, in order to keep in power, it is necessary to build up a powerful machine; one strong enough to crush all opposition and silence all vigorous murmurs of discontent, or the party machine might be smashed and the party thereby lose control.

When I came to realize the faults, failings, shortcomings, aspirations and ambitions of fallible man, I concluded that it would not be the safest nor best policy for society, as a whole, to entrust the management of all its affairs, with all their manifold deviations and ramifications in the hands of finite man, to be managed by the party which happened to come into power, and therefore was the majority party, nor did it then, nor does it now make one particle of difference to me what a party out of power may promise; it does not tend to allay my fears of a party, when intrenched and securely seated in power, might do to crush opposition, and silence the voice of the minority, and thus retard the onward step of progress.

My mind is appalled at the thought of a political party having control of all the details that go to make up the sum total of our lives. Think of it for an instant, that the party in power shall have all authority to dictate the kind of books that shall be used in our schools and universities; government officials editing, printing, and circulating our literature, histories, magazines and press, to say nothing of the thousand and one activities of life that a people engage in, in a civilized society.

To my mind, the struggle for liberty is too great and the few steps we have gained have been won at too great a sacrifice, for the great mass of the people of this twentieth century to consent to turn over to any political party the management of our social and industrial affairs. For all who are at all familiar with history know that men will abuse power when they possess it. For these and other reasons, I, after careful study, and not through sentiment, turned from a sincere, earnest, political Socialist to the non-political phase of Socialism—Anarchism—because in its philosophy I believe I can find the proper conditions for the fullest development of the individual units in society, which can never be the case under government restrictions.

The philosophy of anarchism is included in the word "Liberty," yet it is comprehensive enough to include all things else that are conducive to progress. No barriers whatever to human progression, to thought, or investigation are placed by anarchism; nothing is considered so true or so certain, that future discoveries may not prove it false; therefore, it has but one infallible, unchangeable motto, "Freedom": Freedom to discover any truth, freedom to develop, to live naturally and fully. Other schools of thought are composed of crystallized ideas—principles that are caught and impaled between the planks of long platforms, and considered too sacred to be disturbed by a close investigation. In all other "issues" there is always a limit; some imaginary boundary line beyond which the searching mind dare not penetrate, lest some pet idea melt into a myth. But anarchism is the usher of science—the master of ceremonies to all forms of truth. It would remove all barriers between the human being and natural development. From the natural resources of the Earth, all artificial restrictions, that the body might be nurtured, and from universal truth, all bars of prejudice and superstition, that the mind may develop symmetrically.

Anarchists know that a long period of education must precede any great fundamental change in society, hence they do not believe in vote-begging or political campaigns, but rather in the development of self-thinking individuals.

We look away from government for relief, because we know that force (legalized) invades the personal liberty of man, seizes upon the natural elements and intervenes between man and natural laws; from this exercise of force through governments flows nearly all the misery, poverty, crime and confusion existing in society.

So, we perceive, there are actual, material barriers blockading the way. These must be removed. If we could hope they would melt away, or be voted or prayed into nothingness, we would be content to wait and vote and pray. But they are like great frowning rocks towering between us and a land of freedom, while the dark chasms of a hard-fought past yawn behind us. Crumbling they may be with their own weight and the decay of time, but to quietly stand under until they fall is to be buried in the crash. There is something to be done in a case like this—the rocks must be removed. Passivity while slavery is stealing over us is a crime. For the moment we must forget that we are anarchists—when the work is accomplished we may forget that we were revolutionists—hence most anarchists believe the coming change can only come through a revolution, because the possessing class will not allow a peaceful change to take place; still we are willing to work for peace at any price, except at the price of liberty.

And what of the glowing beyond that is so bright that those who grind the faces of the poor say it is a dream? It is no dream, it is the real, stripped of brain-distortions materialized into thrones and scaffolds, mitres and guns. It is nature acting on her own interior laws as in all her other associations. It is a return to first principles; for were not the land, the water, the light, all free before governments took shape and form? In this free state we will again forget to think of these things as "property." It is real, for we, as a race, are growing up to it. The idea of less restriction and more liberty, and a confiding trust that nature is equal to her work, is permeating all modern thought.

From the dark years—not so long gone by—when it was generally believed that man's soul was totally depraved and every human impulse bad; when every action, every thought and every emotion was controlled and restricted; when the human frame, diseased, was bled, dosed, suffocated and kept as far from nature's remedies as possible; when the mind was seized upon and distorted before it had time to evolve a natural thought—from those days to these years the progress of this idea has been swift and steady. It is becoming more and more apparent that in every way we are "governed best where we are governed least."

Still unsatisfied perhaps, the inquirer seeks for details, for ways and means, and whys and wherefores. How will we go on like human beings—eating and sleeping, working and loving, exchanging and dealing—without government? So used have we become to "organized authority" in every department of life that ordinarily we cannot conceive of the most commonplace avocations being carried on without their interference and "protection." But anarchism is not compelled to outline a complete organization of a free society. To do so with any assumption of authority would be to place another barrier in the way of coming generations. The best thought of today may become the useless vagary of tomorrow, and to crystallize it into a creed is to make it unwieldy.

We judge from experience that man is a gregarious animal, and instinctively affiliates with his kind—cooperates, unites in groups, works to better advantage combined with his fellow man than when alone. This would point to the formation of cooperative communities, of which our present trades-unions are embryonic patterns. Each branch of industry will no doubt have its own organization, regulations, leaders, etc.; it will institute methods of direct communication with every member of that industrial branch in the world, and establish equitable relations with all other branches. There would probably be conventions of industry which delegates would attend, and where they would transact such business as was necessary, adjourn and from that moment be delegates no longer, but simply members of a group. To remain permanent members of a continuous congress would be to establish a power that is certain sooner or later to be abused.

No great, central power, like a congress consisting of men who know nothing of their constituents' trades, interests, rights or duties, would be over the various organizations or groups; nor would they employ sheriffs, policemen, courts or jailors to enforce the conclusions arrived at while in session. The members of groups might profit by the knowledge gained through mutual interchange of thought afforded by conventions if they choose, but they will not be compelled to do so by any outside force.

Vested rights, privileges, charters, title deeds, upheld by all the paraphernalia of government—the visible symbol of power—such as prison, scaffold and armies, will have no existence. There can be no privileges bought or sold, and the transaction kept sacred at the point of the bayonet. Every man will stand on an equal footing with his brother in the race of life, and neither chains of economic thralldom nor menial drags of superstition shall handicap the one to the advantage of the other.

Property will lose a certain attribute which sanctifies it now. The absolute ownership of it—"the right to use or abuse"—will be abolished, and possession, use, will be the only title. It will be seen how impossible it would be for one person to "own" a million acres of land, without a title deed, backed by a government ready to protect the title at all hazards, even to the loss of thousands of lives. He could not use the million acres himself, nor could he wrest from its depths the possible resources it contains.

People have become so used to seeing the evidences of authority on every hand that most of them honestly believe that they would go utterly to the bad it if were not for the policeman's club or the soldier's bayonet. But the anarchist says, "Remove these evidences of brute force, and let man feel the revivifying influences of self-responsibility and self-control, and see how we will respond to these better influences."

The belief in a literal place of torment has nearly melted away; and instead of the direful results predicted, we have a higher and truer standard of manhood and womanhood. People do not care to go to the bad when they find they can as well as not. Individuals are unconscious of their own motives in doing good. While acting out their natures according to their surroundings and conditions, they still believe they are being kept in the right path by some outside power, some restraint thrown around them by church or state. So the objector believes that with the right to rebel and secede, sacred to him, he would forever be rebelling and seceding, thereby creating constant confusion and turmoil.

Is it probable that he *would*, merely for the reason that he *could* do so? Men are to a great extent creatures of habit, and grow to love associations; under reasonably good conditions, he would remain where he commences, if he wished to, and, if he did not, who has any natural right to force him into relations distasteful to him? Under the present order of affairs, persons do unite with societies and remain good, disinterested members for life, where the right to retire is always conceded.

What we anarchists contend for is a larger opportunity to develop the units in society, that mankind may possess the right as a sound being to develop that which is broadest, noblest, highest and best, unhandicapped by any centralized authority, where he shall have to wait for his permits to be signed, sealed, approved and handed down to him before he can engage in the active pursuits of life with his fellow beings. We know that after all, as we grow more enlightened under this larger liberty, we will grow to care less and less for that exact distribution of material wealth, which, on our greed-nurtured senses, seems now so impossible to think upon carelessly. The man and woman of loftier intellects, in the present, think not so much of the riches to be gained by their efforts as of the good they can do for their fellow creatures.

There is an innate spring of healthy action in every human being who has not been crushed and pinched by poverty and drudgery from before his birth, that impels him onward and upward. He cannot be idle, if he would; it is as natural for him to develop, expand, and use the powers within him when not repressed, as it is for the rose to bloom in the sunlight and fling its fragrance on the passing breeze.

The grandest works of the past were never performed for the sake of money. Who can measure the worth of a Shakespeare, a Michelangelo or Beethoven in dollars and cents? Agassiz said, "he had no time to make money"; there were higher and better objects in life than that. And so will it be when humanity is once relieved from the pressing fear of starvation, want, and slavery, it will be concerned, less and less, about the ownership of vast accumulations of wealth. Such possessions would be but an annoyance and trouble. When two or three or four hours a day of easy, of healthful labor will produce all the comforts and luxuries one can use, and the opportunity to labor is never denied, people will become indifferent as to who owns the wealth they do not need.

Wealth will be below par, and it will be found that men and women will not accept it for pay, or be bribed by it to do what they would not willingly and naturally do without it. Some higher incentive must, and will, supersede the greed for gold. The involuntary aspiration born in man to make the most of one's self, to be loved and appreciated by one's fellow-beings, to "make the world better for having lived in it," will urge him on to nobler deeds than ever the sordid and selfish incentive of material gain has done.

If, in the present chaotic and shameful struggle for existence, when organized society offers a premium on greed, cruelty, and deceit, men can be found who stand aloof and almost alone in their determination to work for good rather than gold, who suffer want and persecution rather than desert principle, who can bravely walk to the scaffold for the good they can do humanity, what may we expect from men when freed from the grinding necessity of selling the better part of themselves for bread? The terrible conditions under which labor is performed, the awful alternative if one does not prostitute talent and morals in the service of Mammon; and the power acquired with the wealth obtained by ever-so-unjust means, combine to make the conception of free and voluntary labor almost an impossible one.

And yet, there are examples of this principle even now. In a well-bred family each person has certain duties, which are performed cheerfully, and are not measured out and paid for according to some predetermined standard; when the united members sit down to the well-filled table, the stronger do not scramble to get the most, while the weakest do without, or gather greedily around them more food than they can possibly consume. Each patiently and politely awaits his turn to be served, and leaves what he does not want; he is certain that when again hungry, plenty of good food will be provided. This principle can be extended to include all society, when people are civilized enough to wish it.

Again, the utter impossibility of awarding to each an exact return for the amount of labor performed will render absolute communism a necessity sooner or later. The land and all it contains, without which labor cannot be exerted, belong to no one man, but to all alike. The inventions and discoveries of the past are the common inheritance of the coming generations; and when a man takes the tree that nature furnished free, and fashions it into a useful article, or a machine perfected and bequeathed to him by many past generations, who is to determine what proportion is his and his alone? Primitive man would have been a week fashioning a rude resemblance to the article with his clumsy tools, where the modern worker has occupied an hour. The finished article is of far more real value than the rude one made long ago, and yet the primitive man toiled the longest and hardest.

Who can determine with exact justice what is each one's due? There must come a time when we will cease trying. The Earth is so bountiful, so generous; man's brain is so active; his hands so restless, that wealth will spring like magic, ready for the use of the world's inhabitants. We will become as much ashamed to quarrel over its possession as we are now to squabble over the food spread before us on a loaded table.

"But all this," the objector urges, "is very beautiful in the far-off future, when we become angels. It would not do now to abolish governments and legal restraints; people are not prepared for it."

This is a question. We have seen, in reading history, that wherever an old-time restriction has been removed, the people have not abused their newer liberty. Once it was considered necessary to compel men to save their souls, with the aid of governmental scaffolds, church racks and stakes. Until the foundation of the American republic it was considered absolutely essential that governments should second the efforts of the church in forcing people to attend the means of grace; and yet it is found that the standard of morals among the masses is raised since they are left free to pray as they see fit, or not at all, if they prefer it. It was believed the chattel slaves would not work if the overseer and whip were removed; they are so much more a source of profit now that ex-slaveowners would not return to the old system if they could.

So many able writers have shown that the unjust institutions which work so much misery and suffering to the masses have their root in governments, and owe their whole existence to the power derived from government, we cannot help but believe that were every law, every title deed, every court, and every police officer or soldier abolished tomorrow with one sweep, we would be better off than now. The actual, material things that man needs would still exist; his strength and skill would remain and his instinctive social inclinations retain their force and the resources of life made free to all the people that they would need no force but that of society and the opinion of fellow beings to keep them moral and upright.

Freed from the systems that made him wretched before, he is not likely to make himself more wretched for lack of them. Much more is contained in the thought that conditions make man what he is, and not the laws and penalties made for his guidance, than is supposed by careless observation. We have laws, jails, courts, armies, guns and armories enough to make saints of us all, if they were the true preventives of crime; but we know they do not prevent crime; that wickedness and depravity exist in spite of them—nay, increase as the struggle between classes grows fiercer, wealth greater and more powerful and poverty more gaunt and desperate.

To the governing class the anarchists say: "Gentlemen, we ask no privilege, we propose no restriction; nor, on the other hand, will we permit it. We have no new shackles to propose, we seek emancipation from shackles. We ask no legislative sanction, for cooperation asks only for a free field and no favors; neither will we permit their interference. It asserts that in freedom of the social unit lies the freedom of the social state. It asserts that in freedom to possess and utilize soil lie happiness and progress and the death of rent. It asserts that order can exist only where liberty prevails, and that progress leads and never follows order. It asserts, finally, that this emancipation will inaugurate liberty, equality, fraternity." That the existing industrial system has outgrown its usefulness—if it ever had any—is, I believe, admitted by all who have given serious thought to this phase of social conditions.

The manifestations of discontent now looming upon every side show that society is conducted on wrong principles and that something has got to be done soon or the wage class will sink into a slavery worse than was the feudal serf. I say to the wage class: Think clearly and act quickly, or you are lost. Strike not for a few cents more an hour, because the price of living will be raised faster still, but strike for all you earn, be content with nothing less.

* * *

Following are definitions which will appear in all of the new standard dictionaries:

Anarchism: The philosophy of a new social order based on liberty unrestricted by man-made law, the theory that all forms of government are based on violence—hence wrong and harmful, as well as unnecessary.

Anarchy: Absence of government; disbelief in and disregard of invasion and authority based on coercion and force; a condition of society regulated by voluntary agreement instead of government.

Anarchist: 1. A believer in anarchism; one opposed to all forms of coercive government and invasive authority. 2. One who advocates anarchy, or absence of government, as the ideal of political liberty and social harmony.

Published as a pamphlet,
circa 1905-1910

ON THE "HARMONY" BETWEEN CAPITAL AND LABOR
Or, The Robber and the Robbed

S ir: Please allow a constant reader of your highly appreciated paper to call the attention of those everlasting croakers about the "harmony of Capital and Labor" to an item clipped from last Sunday's *Times*, as follows:

> After a week of opportunity for the glass-pressers to reconsider their action inaugurating a strike because the manufacturers wished to manage their factories according to their own notion [in other words, to break up their Union] eleven of their flint-glass houses finally, today, extinguished fires, and the lockout will be a long one.

Does it need, to the thoughtful-minded, any more convincing proof or stronger argument than the above against the possibility of harmony existing between capital and labor under the present arrangement of the industrial system—or that their interest can, in any way, be "identical"?

If there had been such a thing possible as the harmony of employer and employed (master and slave) would there, to be consistent, *could* there ever have been such a thing as a "strike," which means a resistance on the part of the oppressed toward the oppressor—a protest, as it were? Now we all know too well the definition of the words harmony and identity, when couched in plain language, to mistake their meaning. And how there can be found so many apparently honest persons among the wage-class who still hold to this absurd doctrine, is to the average mind simply a phenomenon.

What harmony 'twixt the oppressor and the oppressed, 'twixt robber and the robbed? Oh, when will ignorance be dethroned, and reason and justice reign supreme? When will the masses learn that property is his and his *only* who has produced it—*earned* it? And that the thieves who prate about "managing their own factories after their own notions" never *earned* one-millionth part of what they now hold and claim as theirs? That it is the unpaid labor of those very thirteen hundred men that they, the thieves, have locked out to *starve*, under the plea of managing their own factories after their own notions!

Let the masses understand that these robbers hold this property (which is so much unpaid labor) under the plea of the laws which they themselves [the robbers] have made, and by the sanction of the very men they have locked out to *starve*; and further, that these so-called laws would not be worth the paper they are written on, twenty-four hours after the producers of all wealth had willed it otherwise.

Oh, when will ignorance be dethroned, and reason and justice reign supreme? When will the masses learn that property is his and his *only* who has produced it—earned it?

Letter to the Editor, The Socialist
December 7, 1878

"RELICS FROM THE LATE CARNAGE":
The New Slavocracy and the Unemployed

The Government [building] rookery is *daily* overrun with a number of mendicants, claiming assistance under the representations that they are relics from the carnage of the late rebellion. These unfortunates, irrespective of the truth or falsity of their representations, are almost invariably referred to some private institution or to the County [poorhouse] authorities, where provision is made for their wants. (From the *Chicago Times*)

The above item is from one of those slandering, venal sheets of this city, whose proprietor had managed to keep far in the rear of cannonballs and bombshells during the late struggle between slavery and freedom, Republican institutions and Slavocracy; who was too great a coward to respond to his country's call in the days of her perilous need to save her from the cruel assaults of a heartless foe. Ah, no! but rather stayed at home, fared sumptuously, and waxed fat on the spoils and "carnage" of a cruel, cruel war; and, in order to prolong the days of the in-flow of his ill-gotten gains at the soldiers' expense, did all in his power

1) to induce the workingman to believe that this was his country; 2) that it was worth saving; 3) that in order to show his patriotism he was in duty bound to forsake family, home and friends, shoulder a musket and make for the front; and 4) should "his country" be wrested from the grasp of a heartless enemy, that he (the soldier) would share in its joys and prosperity as he had in its gloom and woe.

And so it was that thousands, yea, tens of thousands of working-men left their all and bravely hastened forward to the defense of what they believed to be *their* country, leaving the slimy cowards at home to furnish paste-bottom boots the while. The soldier fought, bled, and died; reclaimed the country, and those who were fortunate enough to return, reasonably expected that she, for whom their life's blood had been shed, would at least, in turn, serve them to the end of obtaining an honest, decent living.

But alas! what must be their heartfelt humiliation and burning indignation when they are denied by a bloated aristocracy, a cruel monied-ocracy, the commonest right that should be accorded the yellow cur that runs the streets—*the right to live!*—and [instead] find themselves alluded to in the columns of a hireling, venal press as "mendicants," "relics from the late carnage," "unfortunates," etc. But then, what else can they expect from

A speculating, thievish clan,
Who rob alike on sea and strand.

Letter to the Editor of *The Socialist*,
Chicago, January 25, 1879

❄

WORKINGWOMEN

To the Editor of *The Socialist*: Believing it to be a principle of human nature for people to want to know what others think of them, I would like, for the benefit of workingwomen especially, to lay before your many readers a few extracts from an article entitled "Hints to Young Housekeepers," printed in *Scribner's Magazine* for January, 1879, as follows:

CHOICE OF SERVANTS
Unless they (the servants) have grown old in your service, it is better that servants should not be over forty, for many reasons. Cooks, chambermaids, and laundresses should be strong and active, wholesome and honest-looking, with clean hands, and no long backs, and reject finery. The better educated are more likely to understand their responsibility, and do their duty. For a waitress, you want good looks, an active and neat person, and quick motion.

ENGAGEMENT OF SERVANTS
After making all inquiries, take the servant upon a week's trial. If not satisfied, extend it to a month, unless she is recommended by someone upon whose word you can depend. No servant has a right to throw a household into disorder by leaving without due notice. Make an agreement with the one you are engaging—in writing, if possible—that she must give you due notice of her departure, or forfeit a week's wages. She should claim the same notice of dismissal, unless for misconduct.

Of course, there is never any "misconduct" on the part of the "mistress," and any claim on the servant looking to a contingency of that kind would be considered the height of impertinence, that could only be appeased by peremptory dismissal, without "recommendation." Still, there is an old adage somewhere, to the effect that "what is sauce for the goose is sauce for the gander." But I will continue to quote:

Never send for a servant who is already in a place (situation) or allow any person to apply to you who has not given due notice to her former mistress. I have known several instances of servants being offered higher wages to leave their "present employer"; it is a kind of burglary, and should be punished.

TREATMENT OF SERVANTS
Require careful performance of their duties, strict obedience to your orders, respectful manners, and willing service. They must have time to do their washing and keep their clothes in order, or

they cannot be clean and tidy. Treat them with kindness, but never with familiarity. If they are sad and moody, take no further notice of it than to suggest (if practicable) that the usual holiday should be taken on that day, rather than on the one appropriated to them. Allow them to see their friends in the evening, not in the daytime, for it interrupts work.

Too many servants is a greater evil than too few. They had better be fully employed than not have enough to do.

DUTIES OF A COOK
If a cook could be persuaded [forced] to wear short clothes, short sleeves, strong shoes, a large apron, and clean collar, she would add much to her comfort and yours.

Now, girls, you can judge of how you are to be fed while in the bondage of aristocracy, for the aforesaid magazine gets it down to a nicety, thus:

A quarter of a pound of tea is sufficient for each person for the week, unless you give coffee, too, when one pound of coffee and half the quantity of tea will be sufficient. A pound of sugar is enough for each servant, a candle a week for each servant's bedroom, and one for the cook for the cellar and closets.

Now, Mr Editor, I should much like to comment on the above audacious and gratuitous advice, but am afraid I have already gotten to the "boiling" space. I am in hopes the above items will draw from some of your many lady readers a far more pungent comment than I am capable of rendering. But if no one else does, I, perhaps, will attempt to analyze a few of them at some future time.

Letter to the Editor of The Socialist,
Chicago, February 1, 1879

OUR CIVILIZATION:
Is It Worth Saving?

Is our civilization of today worth saving? might we be asked by the disinherited of the earth. In one respect 'tis a great civilization. History fails to record any other age like ours. When we wish to travel we fly, as it were, on the wings of space, and with a wantonness that would have sunk the wildest imagination of the gods of the ancients into insignificance. We annihilate time. We stand upon the verge of one continent, and converse with ease and composure with friends in the midst of the next. The awe-inspiring phenomena of nature concern us in this age but little. We have stolen the lightning from the gods and made it an obedient servant to the will of man; have pierced the clouds and read the starry page of time.

We build magnificent piles of architecture, whose dizzy heights dazzle us as we attempt to follow with our eye along up the towering walls of solid brick, granite and iron, where tier after tier is broken only by wondrous panes of plate glass. And as we gradually bring the eye down story after story until it reaches the ground, we discover within the very shadow of these magnificent abodes the houseless man, the homeless child, the young girl offering her virtue for a few paltry dollars to hire a little room away up in the garret of one of them. And in the dark recesses of these beautiful buildings the "tramp," demoralized by poverty and abashed by want, attempts to slink from the sight of his fellow beings.

Yet it was their labor that erected these evidences of civilization. Then why are they compelled to be barbarians? For it is labor, and labor only, which makes civilization possible. 'Tis labor that toils, and spins, and weaves, and builds, that another, not it, may enjoy. 'Tis the laborers who dive into the unknown caverns of the sea and compel her to yield up her hidden treasures, which they know not even the value thereof. 'Tis labor which goes into the trackless wilderness, and wields the magic wand which science has placed in its hand. Its hideous, hissing monsters soon succumb, and she blossoms like the rose.

Labor only can level the mountain to the plain, or raise the valley to the mountain height, and dive into the bowels of the earth

44

and bring forth the hidden treasures there contained, which have been latent through the changing cycles of time, and with cunning hand fashion them into articles of use and luxury for the delight and benefit of mankind.

Now, why does this important factor in the arts of progress and refinement continue to hold a secondary position in all the higher and nobler walks of life? Is it not that a few idlers may riot in luxury and ease—said few having dignified themselves "upper classes"?

It is this "upper class" which determines what kind of houses (if any at all) the producing class shall live in, the quantity and quality of food they shall place upon their table, the kind of raiment they shall wear, and whether the child of the proletariat shall in tender years enter the schoolhouse or the factory.

And when the proletariat, failing to see the justice of this bourgeois economy, begins to murmur, the policeman's club is called into active service for six days in the week, while on the seventh the minister assures him that to complain of the powers that be is quite sinful, besides being a losing game, inasmuch as by this action he is lessening his chance for obtaining a very comfortable apartment in "the mansions eternal in the skies." And the possessing class meanwhile are perfectly willing to pay the minister handsomely, and furnish the proletariat all the credit necessary for this if he will furnish them the cash for the erection of their mansions here.

Oh, working man! Oh, starved, outraged, and robbed laborer, how long will you lend attentive ear to the authors of your misery? When will you become tired of your slavery and show the same by stepping boldly into the arena with those who declare that "Not to be a slave is to dare and DO?" When will you tire of such a civilization and declare in words, the bitterness of which shall not be mistaken, "Away with a civilization that thus degrades me; it is not worth the saving?"

Chicago, The Alarm, August 8, 1885

A CHRISTMAS STORY

And here is my mail with a letter from Santa Claus who has not even forgotten me, although the halcyon days of childhood's sweet delusion have long since vanished from me. And the precious missive which the venerable old sire in his rambles through foreign lands has found and brought to me, becomes so interesting as I peruse its contents that I have determined to let the readers of *The Alarm* have the benefit of it.

The story is laid in a barbarous isle, and is the result of the very sudden advent of a ship-wrecked Christian, who in return for the many kindnesses which he has received at the hands of his new neighbors, proposes to carry a few of them back with him to his own country that he may show them the benefits of a Christian civilization in order that the benighted barbarian may return to his own country and become a missionary in the cause of Christian civilization and a good government.

The little missive which Santa Claus has so kindly brought me seems to be a report of those missionaries made upon their return to their native country. The report says:

"They carried us in an easterly direction across the angry waves of the mighty ocean on the wings of a huge and beautiful sea bird (they called it a steamship) and landed us upon the verge of a great continent where nature seemed to always smile. And when we alighted from our lovely sea bird we were placed behind a horse of steel who blew and neighed and panted, impatient to start on his long journey across the wide expanding continent, and when at last he was started, he carried us with lightning speed; he whirled through valleys, across plains, and climbed the mountainside with all the ease of a giant that he was, never tiring, never flagging, but always reaching out as if in search of more land to cover; time seemed to dwindle before his onward strides, and space was annihilated."

A voice in the audience inquired: "How could he hold out?"

"Oh, he was driven by steam, a discovery which they claimed was the most wonderful ever made since their God had made the world."

The missionary continued to read the report: "On the fifth day after our starting they landed us in the heart of a magnificent city. This was about 10 o'clock a.m., and the people whom we saw moving about in such apparent ease, driving about the avenues of wealth and marts of trade in magnificent equipages, arrayed in costliest raiment, our guide informed us, were the sole owners of all those enormous structures which so amazed us; that they were in fact the sole possessors of the earth and all it contained, and lived but to enjoy. In our admiration we exclaimed, 'Mighty is the Christian Civilization! Great is their government!' [Great sensation in the audience, and cries of 'Let's emigrate.']

"Hold on, comrades, hear us through," said the missionary, resuming: "We were shown all the wonderful sights in the arts and methods of warfare, and promised to be shown those of industry of this Christian people. We were conducted into marble halls where banquet boards were spread and lovely women came and went, fairy-like, all bespangled with precious jewels and gems of greatest worth. Their fair faces fairly beamed with contentment, ease and happiness." [Murmur in the audience: 'Mighty is the Christian Civilization!']

"As night grew on apace and sparkling wine from vine-wreathed cups was freely drunk, and toasts in quick succession were freely and hilariously offered, which ran about thus: 'Happy, contented, and prosperous are our people under the benign influence of a wisely managed and Christian Government,' and as the applause from the last toast echoed along down the granite columns of the banqueting hall which made the silken draperies quiver and fairly rent the magnificent frescoed ceiling, a strange apparition appeared and stood about midway in the hall so that none could help but see it.

"That apparition was the wretchedest of women. And from her cavernous eyes, pale flashes seemed to rise, as when the northern skies gleamed in December. And like the water's flow under December snow came a dull voice of woe from the heart's chamber:

'Ladies and gentlemen, Christian people,' said she, 'while at your banqueting board will you hear the prayer of the widow, the cry of the orphan? Without, the blinding snow falls thick and fast. Three months ago this day I, for the fifth time, became a mother, and on that very day I was made a widow and they were orphaned

47

by my poor husband being crushed to a shapeless mass among the machinery in that man's factory (pointing to the proposer of the last toast) and I swear to you that twice these twelve hours past we have been without a morsel of food or a bit of fuel, and I am afraid to return to my wretched hovel for fear they have already perished from cold and hunger. Oh! In God's name hear their cries if not mine!'

For a moment all seemed transfixed; then a slight noise was heard, when from a recess emerged an officious person all done up in a large blue coat with brass buttons and quickly stepping up to the apparition, drew the thin, faded shawl over the pale, haggard cheeks and flashing eyes, thus stifling the cries for 'mercy.'

Voices from the audience: "Didn't the Christians say anything?"

"Yes, they spoke for a few moments in whispers."

"What did they say?"

"Well, from the ladies side could be heard sentences like these: 'Pshaw! Such management, as to let such a creature make her way into the banqueting hall, and especially when strangers are present.'

"Another lady of very matronly appearance spoke thus: 'Oh! Did you hear the language she used about becoming a mother? Just as though we care how many brats she had or when they were born.'

"From the gentlemen we could hear expressions like these: 'Those fancied grievances from the improvident lower classes, in venting their supposed wrongs and annoying decent people, is becoming altogether too frequent. We must have the military well practiced in 'street riot drill,' and equipped so as to be ready to quell the first manifestation of an attempt on their part to force a recognition of the 'justness' of 'righting their alleged wrongs.'

Other gentlemen said: 'Yes, yes, you are right. We have been reading the *Tribune*'s appeal to businessmen after the Thanksgiving Day street riot drill, and I have myself been soliciting contributions from among the propertied classes, with no small success.'

"These, and many more expressions of a like tenor could be heard from all present.

"The time having now arrived for leave-taking and a pleasant good-night, we soon left the room, and as myself and guide

48

emerged from the magnificent building, our host seemed completely lost in praise of the 'prosperity and hospitality of a Christian people.'

"We were about to take a cab, when my attention was attracted, and I stopped, with one foot upon the cab step, and as I did so, I discerned several of the brass-buttoned fellows before referred to forcing along as many young girls, who were weeping and declaring they would not have been 'soliciting' upon the street if they had not been driven to do so. One said her aged mother was without 'food or fuel,' and another said, 'Oh, sir, please, please let me go just this time. I swear to you I have been trying so hard to get work, but I could not, and now my landlord has served notice upon me, and myself and little children will be thrown upon the street if the rent is not paid tomorrow.'

"On my turning to our friend, he guessed the question I was about to ask, and with an impatient wave of the hand, informed us that these persons 'were only a lot of unfortunate creatures whom we in this Christian country turn over to the authorities to be dealt with. In fact, that is mainly what we have our government for, the taking charge of the lower classes.'

"When the Sabbath bells pealed out calling these Christians to their gorgeous temples to worship their gods, we, too, were escorted to one of them, and introduced to the minister in charge as some 'heathen who had been induced to come among us to learn the habits of a God-fearing people, that they might learn the ways of the Christian, in order that they might return to their own land and become missionaries.' The minister very sanctimoniously declared that 'we are faithful followers of the meek and lowly Jesus, who had nowhere to lay his head,' then mounted his gorgeous pulpit and took for his text words to this effect: 'That it was as difficult for a rich man to enter the kingdom of heaven as for a camel to go through the eye of a needle, unless they were very generous to the poor,' and when the contribution box was passed around it was very generously remembered.

"One fine day, after we had been in the Christian country but a few weeks, we strolled down in the midst of the marts of trade, and as we stood and gazed in wonderment and admiration at the towering buildings, these same buildings seemed to suddenly begin to take on a different aspect, as we heard the great clock in the tower begin to strike the hour of six, and as it did so there began to stream out from all these monstrous buildings a blackening stream of people, who, as they came forth, seemed to be hurrying helter skelter in every direction, as though their very life depended upon their getting somewhere in the shortest time imaginable. These people seemed so different from those whom we had been accustomed to seeing. These last were pale-faced, care-worn and hard-worked people, who seemed to have no time nor desire to stop and enjoy the beautiful displays in the show windows as the well-dressed ones whom we had during the day seen doing so; and in this struggling mass of hurrying humanity we could see little children of tender age looking as over-worked as those more mature in years.

"While we were peering into these people's faces, trying to make out why it was they looked so different from those whom we had seen at church and at the banquet, just then our guide stepped up and told us that these people whom we now saw were 'only the working class; the lower element in our society.'

"'Working people, did you say?' we asked. 'Then do they not build those beautiful buildings which they are coming out of?'

"Oh, yes; we have them do the work, but we superintend it."

"Then of course they own them?"

"No. You see, it is like this: these people are the working class. It is the capitalists who own the property."

"Then, if these people are the working people as you say they are, why is it they are not owners of this property?"

"Well, you see, it is very difficult for the heathen to understand the political economy of a Christian civilization. You see, it is like this: we employ these classes and pay them so much of their labor product, which we call wages; and of course this is a great blessing to them, for if they were not so employed by us they could not obtain the comforts of life they now enjoy."

"'But are they satisfied to simply receive wages for their work? Do they quietly submit?"

"No, not always; but we do not permit any interference on their part; we deal with them summarily." [A voice in the audience: 'What do you think of the Christian government and their boasted

50

civilization?']

"What do we think of it? Why, from what we could learn of their government it is simply organized fraud and oppression; because if their people are happy and contented as they claim, then what do they need to be governed for? And in their religion they are hypocrites, inasmuch as they preach one thing and practice another.

"And in their economical or industrial system they are robbers, fleecing old and young alike, and under the shadow of their altars they keep great engines of destruction that they may send their enemies to hell by the wholesale. As for my part, I move that we send missionaries among them at once, not to teach them how to die, but how to live; not to be soul-savers but body-savers. Teach them how not to make criminals of the people by overwork and poverty that their ministers may have a job praying them out of hell!"

In the midst of the great sensation and commotion which arose at this motion and the cries of "second the motion," and "send missionaries at once!"—amid all this confusion Santa Claus seems to have lost part of the manuscript of this very interesting report, and the readers of *The Alarm* will have to be content with what is here given.

The Alarm, December 26, 1885

THE HAYMARKET MEETING:
A Graphic Description of the Attack
on that Peaceable Assembly

The following letter was written when all the events of that terrible night were fresh in my memory—in fact were burning in my soul, when the awful detonation was still ringing in my ears and police outrages were occurring all around me—in fact in my own home.

51

The readers of the *Enquirer* have read with bated breath the startling news flashed from this city on Tuesday last of the ushering in and demonstration of the new method of scientific warfare. What was it, and what the occasion of the bringing forth of the fell destroyer from his lurking-place in the realms of science with such direful results? The cause may be given in a future letter, the results may be given here.

The minions of the oppressing class were marching up to one of the most peaceably assembled meetings ever held in this country by any class of people to discuss questions concerning their own interests, and commanded them to "disperse." The individual giving this order was backed by about 300 armed and bludgeon-wielding police, whom the capitalistic press described as having "grasped their clubs tighter as they came in sight of the Anarchists assembled."

Well, as the minions moved from the station, which was half a block away from the meeting, they came like a lowering cloud to blot out the sunlight of free speech on American soil. Sweeping from curbstone to curbstone (a new military tactic which they had been practicing for some time especially for the Anarchists), and stepping with military precision and unbroken ranks, each one "grasping tightly his club," compelled the people peaceably assembled there to fall back upon the sidewalk. When the three first columns had moved past the speakers' stand, a halt was called. The individual referred to commanded these peaceable people to "disperse." The reply was given in thunder tones, which shook the great massive buildings for blocks around. A great swath had been cut in the ranks of the police. But before their groans, mingled with the succeeding echoes of the great explosion, could rise, as it were, from the place where they originated, there came a fusillade of pistol-shots. The bomb had been flung with such sudden and deadly effect that it had thoroughly disorganized and demoralized the police, and they became an easy prey for an enemy to attack and completely annihilate, if there had been any conspiracy or concocted understanding, as has been howled and shouted by the capitalistic press.

It was the shortest, sharpest, and most decisive battle, I believe, on record. In less than three minutes the most horrible explosion ever known of its kind had taken place, over two hundred shots had been fired and over fifty police lay writhing in their blood upon the ground. The 3,000 or more persons who had been assembled on the spot less than an hour previous—where were they? For nothing now was to be heard or seen but the writhing, groaning police, and citizens whose names were never known, and the coming and going of the patrol, each loaded with victims and conveying them to hospitals.

Since that date a reign of terror has been inaugurated which would put to shame the most zealous Russian bloodhound. The organized banditti and conscienceless brigands of capital have suspended the only papers which would give the side of those whom they had crammed into prison cells. They have invaded the homes of everyone who has ever been known to have raised a voice or sympathized with those who have had aught to say against the present system of robbery and oppression. I say they have invaded their homes and subjected them and their families to indignities that must be seen to be believed. This organized banditti have arrested me four times; they have subjected me to indignities that should bring the tinge of shame to the calloused cheek of a hardened barbarian.

But evidently becoming convinced that I had nothing to "give away," they have ceased to drag me to the station, for the time at least. But my comrades need have no concern lest these ruffians should, by their brutal treatment of me, drive me to distraction. They simply challenge my contempt.

All we in Chicago ask of our comrades abroad is to withhold their opinion until they hear our side, and to furnish us such moral and financial aid as they can.

Written in Chicago, May 10, 1886, this letter appeared in various papers; it is reprinted here from *The Liberator*, November 11, 1905

THE NEGRO:
Let Him Leave Politics to the Politician and Prayers to the Preacher

Who has stood upon the seashore and watched the weird dash of the ceaseless waves and has not become tired of their monotonous sameness? Still there was occasionally a wave which could attract and fix our attention for the time being by rearing its cap above the rest and thus become conspicuous.

Who but a devoted soul in this labor movement does not at times become tired—a weary tiredness, verging on a disgust at the apparent sameness and dreary monotony of the wage system as depicted by those engaged in the noble work of exposing the hideous inequalities of the present economic system? Yet, like the waves, there arises amid all this monotony a wrong sometimes as much or more glaring in all its details that not only is our attention attracted but our sympathies are enlisted.

Who, surrounded even as we are in the midst of organizations whose mission it is to depict the wrongs to which the propertyless class are subjected, could help but stand aghast and heave a sigh and perchance drop a tear as they read the graphic account flashed to us of the awful massacre of the poor and defenseless wage-slaves in Carrolton, in the state of Mississippi? Defenseless, poverty-stricken, hemmed about by their deadly enemies; victims not only to their misfortunes, but to deep-seated, blind, relentless prejudice, these our fellow-beings are murdered without quarter.

This is the history in brief: The plain unvarnished facts of this most damnable outrage which, with it and similar occurrences almost innumerable of a like nature perpetrated upon these people, should bring a tinge of indignation to the cheek of every soul who can at all comprehend the meaning of the word Liberty!

While these are the plain facts, what is the lesson it teaches? Are there any so stupid as to believe these outrages have been, are being and will be heaped upon the Negro because he is black? Not at all. It is because he is poor. It is because he is dependent. Because he is poorer as a class than his white wage-slave brother of the North.

And to the Negro himself we would say your deliverance lies mainly in your own hands. You are the modern Helot. You sow but another reaps. You till the soil but for another to enjoy. Who is this other one who continues to enjoy the fruit of your industry? Are they not the idle few who you but lately acknowledged as your masters, and are not these loafers practically your masters yet in so far as absorbing all your labor product without even being compelled to return you sufficient to keep you in decent food and clothes? For they are not even actuated by the monied interest which they had in you in former years. The overseer's whip is now fully supplanted by the lash of hunger! And the auction block by the chain-gang and convict cell!

The same land which you once tilled as a chattel slave you still till as a wage-slave, and in the same cabin which you then entered at eve not knowing but what you would be sold from wife and little ones before the morrow's setting sun, you now enter with dread lest you will be slain by the assassin hand of those who once would simply have sold you if they did not like you.

Verily your situation is still deplorable. Will the soft, smooth words of the bidder for your vote emancipate you from these conditions? Who has tried the delusive thing more faithfully than you have? Has it done you any good? Will prayer stay the hand of the oppressor? Who has prayed with more zeal than you? Of what practical good has it ever been to you? Then clearly your road to redemption lies not along these paths. But your course in future, if you value real freedom, is to leave politics to the politician, and prayer to those who can show wherein it has done them more good than it has ever done for you, and join hands with those who are striving for economic freedom.

Can you divine what this freedom means? Homes for the homeless producer of today, and only those who produce shall have them, and no longer shall the industrious many feed the idle few, who riot in luxury and ease.

As to those local, periodical, damnable massacres to which you are at all times liable, these you must revenge in your own way. Are you deaf, dumb and blind to the atrocities that you are subjected to? Have the gaping wounds of your dying comrades become so common that they no longer move you? Is your heart a heart of stone, or its palpitations those of cowards, that you slink to your wretched abode and offer no resistance? Do you need something to nerve you to action? Then look in the tear-stained eye of your sorrowing wife and hungry children, or think of your son, who has been sent to the chain-gang or perhaps murdered upon your door-steps. Do you need more horrible realities than these to goad you on to deeds of revenge that will at least make your oppressors dread you? And this is the beginning of respect! Do you ask me what I would do if I were like you, poor, unarmed and defenseless? You are not absolutely defenseless.

For the torch of the incendiary, which has been known to show murderers and tyrants the danger line, beyond which they may not venture with impunity, cannot be wrested from you.

The Alarm, 3 April 1886

CHALLENGING THE LYING MONOPOLISTIC PRESS:
A Letter to Joseph Labadie*

Cincinnati, Ohio, October 11, 1886

Dear Comrade: I am meeting with success far beyond what the comrades here expected. I addressed a large and enthusiastic meeting here on Sunday the 10th and will address one tonight, and the prospects are good for a still larger one. The noticeable feature about that meeting was that it was composed almost entirely of conservative trade unionists who applauded my utterances to the echo, and accepted my definition of the red flag with *rapture.* Ah! I tell you the people are becoming hungry for the other side of the late judicial farce known as the Anarchist trial.

I go from here to Louisville, thence to Cleveland, and to New York City, Pittsburgh, Pennsylvania, etc. You know, comrade, that my present trip is for the purpose of enlightening the American people upon this all-important judicial murdering operation in Chicago and to raise funds for the defense.

I am not afraid to trust to the common sense of the American people in deciding upon any case when both sides are heard, and giving their verdict of guilt where it *belongs*.

If the great body of the people have clamored for our comrades' blood, it was because they believed what the lying monopolistic press has said. Now let them be just as anxious to hear the other side, and I have no fear of the verdict in the case, when the people sit as jurors.

Yours for emancipated labor,
Lucy E. Parsons

Labadie Collection, University of Michigan Library, Ann Arbor

WHAT ANARCHY MEANS

There is no picture so dark but has its bright side—no life so dreary but what at some time a ray of hope flits across its cheerless path. There is no movement so heinous (?) but to those engaged in it has its amusing side. But who can assume for one moment that the awful, horrible, anarchistic movement of "blood-drinking" anarchists can have any amusing side to it? How could such "fiends" ever smile? For after reading insinuations from the pulpit, assertions from the press, and "criticisms" from professional critics, to the average reader an avowed anarchistic society must be composed of beings somewhat resembling the human family, who hold orgies, which they designate as meetings; having been compelled to come in contact with the human race enough (just enough) to learn a few words of their language.

Places selected for holding said meetings (orgies) by these "anarchist fiends" are in keeping with all the rest of their diabolisms, inasmuch as they invariably select only places that are dark, dank and loathsome, where no light is ever permitted to penetrate, either of sunlight or intelligence. And at such appointed times and places these "hysterics of the labor movement" (for these "fiends" have deluded themselves into the belief that they have something in common with the labor movement) write their diabolical mandates upon grimy tables covered with bomb-slaughtered capitalists, these "fiends" having improved upon the capitalist method of starving said victims, and then taking their hides to make fine slippers for their daughters, etc.

And as these "foul conspirators" each in turn reaches a mangy hand under the table and takes therefrom a capitalistic infant's skull, each slowly raises bloodshot eyes, fills said skull with sour beer, and clinks the same with some fellow- conspirator's sour beer which is contained in the empty half of a dynamite bomb. At this signal, the whole crowd arise and straighten, as well as they can, their tatterdemalion forms, and with distended nostrils hiss from between clenched teeth, "BLOOD!"

Now, I will ask the readers of *The Advance* and the reading public if the above picture is at all overdrawn when compared with articles from the press, both so-called religious and secular, and also of insinuations from the pulpit for the last few months, regarding that class of people designated anarchist?

The amusing part of this business to the average anarchist is just here—*i.e.*, that we are being used just now as a kind of a bugaboo, a scarecrow to frighten the capitalists into certain concessions to their rebellious slaves, otherwise said slaves might become "anarchist fiends." And this little game is being played for all its worth by certain labor "reformers" and especially by the church. But the capitalists don't frighten a dollar's worth.

In substantiation of a thousand illustrations coming under the observation of anarchists all the time, I need here but note a few, and these from the pulpit. The Rev. Hugh O. Pentecost,* of the Congregational church, Newark, N.J., in his sermon entitled the "Henry George Solution of the Labor Problem," as reported in the *New York Standard*, says:

> If you say that Henry George is an anarchist, you will simply be exposing your own ignorance. A man who writes two or three

books of a purely philosophical character is not an anarchist. A book is not an anarchist's instrument. Before you pronounce judgment on a man you want to hear what that man has to say.

Wonder if the most Rev. D.D. has ever heard of Reclus, Kropotkin, Bakunin, Proudhon, Marx, Fourier and a host of other renowned anarchists who have written books of "a purely philosophical character"? From the same sermon I take this extract:

> The Roman Catholic church has made a big mistake in opposing the Knights of Labor. I have studied the Knights of Labor for several years, and I have become convinced that the organization is one of the great bulwarks that stand between society and red-handed anarchism.

Does this reverend gentleman throw this out as sop to capitalists? Yes, "bulwarks," "red-handed anarchism," etc. Well, it won't work, because the twenty-one demands of the Knights of Labor platform are an endeavor to supplant the present wage system by a system of cooperation and my dear friend, "red-handed anarchism," where and when the wage system has ended. Every attempt of labor organizations to improve the condition of the wage-worker, is—when successful—a limitation of the capitalist's power (authority) and a limitation of the severities of the wage-system.

The capitalist understands full well that his power consists solely of his privilege to dictate the terms and conditions to those who bring to him their commodity-labor-for-sale, and any organization, it matters not under what name, which attempts in any way to limit or deny this privilege, *viz*: the power of the possessing class over the non-possessing producing class, is met by the lockout, the blacklist, and when necessary, the policeman's club and the militiaman's bayonet. And this is all justified upon the right of the employer's "conducting his business to suit himself."

Now these are potent facts, which no one having eyes to see can deny, and to assume for one moment that capital and labor (or capitalists and laborers) have an identity of interest, is to assume that the purchaser and seller of a pair of boots have an identity of interest. The one has something to sell, the other to buy. The one's interest is to get all he can, the other's to give just as little as possible. And this commodity—labor—is controlled the same as any other article, *viz*: by the amount to be found in the market.

Hence it is the capitalistic class always in all countries, who strive and manage to keep an army of laborers in compulsory idleness, to be moved around to take the place of any "kickers" in that very "bulwark" which is to stand between them and "red-handed anarchism."

Again the reverend gentleman says:

> The Knights of Labor imagine that they are tyrannized over, and once in a while they will do things no one will commend them for. It is this system. A great many think the troubles arise from employers. I know some that are as good as any men who walk the face of the earth. There are some hard-hearted employers, but they are not at the bottom of the trouble. It is on account of the system.

Yes, I presume it is only imagination (?) on the part of the K. of L. that they are "tyrannized over." But it is the "system," says the reverend gentleman, which is at fault. What more has any anarchist said? Evidently, the reverend gentleman, like many others, is an anarchist and doesn't know it. But you just touch this beautiful wage system and see under what head capital will place you. And as to those "good employers," so too there were good chattel slave masters, but what did that have to do with the system of chattel slavery, except to prolong its existence by having the good slave masters held up as shining examples to prove the harmony (?) existing between master and slave, which the horrible abolitionist would sever, just as is the case today with those relations between "good" employers and the wage-slaves, which the "red-handed anarchist" is seeking to destroy. But the anarchists simply answer with the Rev. D.D., "it is the system which is at fault."

Well, if it is the system that is at the bottom of the trouble, then it certainly should follow to the average thinking person that the system must be changed. But this reverend gentleman durst not propose such a remedy to his congregation, else he might be set down as a "disturber of the peace," just as though anything in the line of justice can be brought about unless the "peace" of established injustice is disturbed!

I will state briefly for the information of those who are so busily engaged just now in declaiming against the system and declaring they are not anarchists in the same breath, that our position is about this, to-wit: The wage-system having outgrown its usefulness, inasmuch as it creates famine in the midst of abundance, and makes slaves of nine-tenths of the human family, that it (the system) must go!

And having read history I can't find any instance where the ruling classes have relinquished any "vested right" without compulsion. And knowing that private property in the means of existence is a "vested right" as much as any ever was or can be, it being upheld by the constitutions of all governments, backed by their powerful armies, we don't believe the privileged class are going peaceably to surrender these "vested rights."

The Advance and Labor Leaf, March 12, 1887; originally titled "We Are All Anarchists"

ARREST IN COLUMBUS, OHIO

Believing that your paper is published in the interest of truth, I ask for space in its columns to state briefly the facts relating to my incarceration in the Columbus prison. The venal capitalistic press has heralded the information all over the country that I was arrested for insulting the Mayor of Columbus. I never insulted the Mayor. My arrest was simply the carrying out of a conspiracy to suppress free speech. The Mayor is reported in the press as saying "he did not propose to have me preach Anarchy in Columbus, which must inevitably lead to bloodshed," and the Mayor said "the meeting is declared off."

In this connection, at this stage, it will be observed that there is no pretense that the hall had been rented under false pretenses. This evidently was an afterthought. As to my preaching "murder and incendiaries" I have this to say: that since the 13th day of last October I have lectured in sixteen States of this Union, as far East as the Atlantic seaboard and as far West as Omaha, and from Milwaukee to Louisville and Baltimore in the South, and during this time, in the course of some fifty-odd lectures, I have addressed near onto 200,000 persons, embracing people in every walk of life, yet in this vast concourse of people there is not one who can truthfully say that I ever uttered one word that could be construed into inciting to the commission of murder or that would bring the tinge to the cheek of the most fastidious.

In my lectures I have simply stated facts as they exist, and it will be a sad day for the American people when they supinely witness the dearest rights known to man stolen from them—rights which the founders of this Government said should not be abridged, not even by act of Congress, viz.: the right to peaceably assemble (stolen from them by the crafty use of the word Anarchy)—for, the precedent once established, the way is easy to dump every popular movement under this head, and thus effectually stifle the people's voice.

But to my subject. On Sunday, March 6, I received a letter stating that a hall had been secured for me to lecture at Columbus, Ohio, and all necessary arrangements made. Acting upon this information, I left Cincinnati on Tuesday, March 8, for Columbus, arriving there at 7 o'clock p.m. Next day, in company with two friends, I walked around the city seeing places of interest. So, remembering I was in the capital of the State of Ohio, I expressed a desire to my friends to visit the halls of legislation.

While we were in the Senate chamber a gentleman entered and informed us that he had heard I would not be permitted to speak in the hall rented for that purpose. At this announcement, as might be imagined, we were much surprised. I suggested to the friends with me that we go and ascertain if there was any foundation for the rumor. So accordingly we went from the State House building to the hall. The janitor stated that he had arranged the chairs in the hall and was putting things in order, but at noon he had received orders to permit no one but members of the State militia in the hall that evening. Upon receiving this information I suggested that we call upon the gentleman from whom the hall had been rented. We repaired to his office. On observing our entrance he became quite angry, and stated that he had rented the hall to the trades association and not to anarchists. The gentleman accompanying us denied that he had represented himself as engaging it for the trades association. I then produced the receipt and showed it to him, and called his attention to the fact that the receipt read that the hall had been rented for March 8 to "association," and that no specified association had been mentioned. He said he didn't care, he was not going to have the anarchists speaking in that hall, etc.; that we could have the money we had paid, but he would see to it that we didn't get the hall. I said:

"Do you mean to say after you have rented me the hall you are going to prevent my using it?"

He said that was just what he meant. Then I said:

"If you understand anarchy to mean violence and disorder, you, sir, are the only anarchist I know of in Columbus just now."

We then left his office and went to the Mayor's office, one block away. As we left, the agent ran upstairs (his office was in the basement) and ordered a policeman, who seemed to be stationed there, to arrest the gentleman, myself and Mrs Lyndall. The policeman rushed up to the man and slapped him on the shoulder, as if to place him under arrest. I said:

"Don't arrest that man. He has done nothing. Besides, we are on our way to the Mayor's office."

The policeman went on with us, and by this time we had arrived at the Mayor's office; Police Court had just adjourned. I was told by one of the officers in the corridor to go into the Mayor's private office; he would be a minute. Maj. Coit, the agent from whom the hall had been rented, had reached the Mayor's office by this time, and had a few moments' private talk with the Mayor. Then the Mayor and about twenty-five police and detectives crowded into the room where myself and Mrs Lyndall were seated.

As soon as the Mayor entered, Mrs Lyndall introduced him to me. I could at once see he was much the worse for drink. I was calm as I ever was in my life, and as politely as I knew how to, I began to address him thus:

"You are the Mayor? Well, sir, I have rented a hall in which to speak tonight, but have been told that I will not be permitted to speak in it. Now, sir, I come to you, as the highest peace officer in this city, to request you to see to it that order is maintained—"

Just at this juncture, and before I could finish my sentence, he broke in, and with a flourish of his hand, said:

"I don't want to hear anything from you. There will be no

meeting in that hall tonight."

My answer to this unexpected rejoinder was this, and only this, the venal press to the contrary notwithstanding:

"Sir, I come to you, not as a dictator, but as a servant of the people," but before I could utter another word he said to the pack of sleuth-hounds (detectives) standing around him:

"Take her down."

I did not know what he meant, but it seems they did, for one weighing about 200 pounds and near six feet tall jumped at and seized me by the arm and called upon another one to take me by the other arm, and as to the way they handled me, my arms bear their fingerprints to this day, and can be seen by any one. I have shown them to my friends, who were moved to tears at the evidences of their brutality, as shown by the black spots on both of my arms. They jerked my shawl off my shoulders and threw it at Mrs Lyndall, and said to her:

"Here, take this!" This was witnessed by at least fifty people in the corridor, not one of whom can truthfully say I was using any language unbecoming a lady. At this juncture, the suddenness of the onslaught and the termination of my interview with the Mayor was so different from what I anticipated, that I think I was more dazed than anything else. But what I do remember saying to those two hulks—who had torn my shawl from my shoulders and thrown it at Mrs Lyndall, as above stated, that they might the better grip my arms as in a vice, and as they dragged me downstairs—was this: "You scoundrels! Does it take two of you to carry one little woman?"

By this time I had been hurried downstairs and the charge of "disorderly conduct" placed opposite my name. And the reader can well imagine that this occurred in ten times less time than it takes to tell it. In fact, it was all over in three minutes.

The place I was put in for the first four hours of my incarceration, I understand from the Columbus papers, is known as the "ranch." The "ranch" I will describe. This "ranch" consists of a long, narrow passageway (about four feet wide and twenty feet long) upon which open heavy iron doors, leading from small, dark, filthy, ill-smelling, dungeonlike cells; in fact, they *are* dungeons. Well, on my being thrust into the narrow passageway above described, and the iron bolt clicked into its place, denoting that I was buried for the time being from the world, the sights I beheld and what I passed through for the next twenty-one hours can never be erased from my memory, though it were possible for me to live a thousand years. I saw lying upon an indescribably filthy semblance of a quilt a young woman, not particularly bad-looking so far as facial expression went. Then sitting about the filthy, hard stone floor were four other females; there was no chair or anything else to sit upon. Standing near the barred window was another rather good-looking young woman, I should say about twenty years old. As soon as the door closed they all began to ply me with questions which ran thus:

"What are you run in for?"

"Disorderly conduct," I answered.

"Is this your first time?"

"Yes," I answered.

"Oh, well, it won't go very hard with you then, if it is the first time."

"How hard do you think it will go with me?" I asked.

"Oh, if it's the first time, $5 and costs, and if you can show you never was in before, it won't be that much."

"Well, do you think I can get out on bail tonight?" I asked.

"Yes, if you have got about $10 to put up, and if you ain't got that much I see you have got a watch. Put that up. But don't let 'em around here know that you've got much money. If you do they will soak you."

The conversation ran on in this strain for a while, until I obtained all the information I wished; then I turned it off by asking them what they got to eat and when they got it. The answer was:

"Bread and water and salt for breakfast, nothing for dinner, and bread and water and salt for supper."

"And is that all you have?"

"Yes," they replied.

"And this is what you have, and you are put in here for punishment. Are you any better off when you go out?"

They all answered in chorus: "Ha! We are a sight worse. It only makes a girl worse to treat them like we are treated."

I then began to look into the filthy, dark, little dungeons, and was about to enter one when they cried out:

"Don't go in there! You'll get full of bedbugs."

"Well, where do you sleep?" I asked.

"Out here on the floor," they answered.

"What, upon this hard, stone floor? Where are your bed-clothes?"

"We don't have any," was the reply.

"What, do you sleep on nothing?"

Some of them began to wish the man would come on around with the bread and salt, as they were getting hungry. I noticed, while engaged in conversation with some, that others were going to the door and talking through a little hole not much larger than a silver dollar, using the vilest language I had ever heard escape from the lips of human beings. About this time a man came to the door and opened it, and asked if we were hungry. I asked the girls if they would like a sandwich. They thanked me, and I sent out for seven —the number present—six besides myself.

Afterwards a guard came to the door and I asked him if there was not some way for me to get out, as I didn't want to stay in that place all night. He said he thought so. I asked him how much would be required. He said $10 was what was usually required, and if I had that amount and would leave it with the desk officer he thought I could get out. I told him I not only had $10, but a $50 watch also, and to go and tell the parties in control I would leave both. I never saw him after.

I had now been in this den (which must be seen to be appreciated) about three hours. During all this time it seemed that all the vile, base, low men in Columbus had been admitted, and peeked in and carried on with the creatures in that den—soldiers from the Barracks included—and the language they used must be heard to be believed. About 10 o'clock p.m., a guard came to the door and ordered me to take my things and follow him.

My "things" consisted of my shawl, which had been snatched from me in the afternoon, and which Mrs Lyndall had returned to me at my request. I was conducted into a narrow cell, or rather dungeon, about five feet long and four feet wide. In this insufferably hot hole I was kept locked until 4 o'clock next day, without one thing to sleep on except some oaken slats which were held together by iron bolts and suspended by iron chains. Mrs Lyndall, when she called the next morning, asked the guard why I was not permitted to come out in the passageway and exercise and have fresh air. The reply was that orders had been given that I was to be kept locked in. None of my friends were permitted to see me all the time I was incarcerated, although some thirty or forty called—none but Mrs Lyndall, who was permitted to bring my meals. But every loafing detective and ward bummer in the city, every disreputable male brute who wished to come and lean against the iron grating of the dark, hot, little sweat box I was locked in could do so.

Whenever a gang of these put in an appearance—gangs numbering never less than three up to ten—the door leading into the passageway containing the dungeon in which I was confined—that great bolt in the other door flew back and they walked in and would leer at me as though I were a wild beast belonging to a menagerie. And they would laugh at me and asked "how much I liked it"; how was my "health." Now this did not happen once, twice, thrice, but there was a continuous throng all the time I was there.

Next day following the one on which I was incarcerated, I was brought into Court, and here I found, in the same individual, complainant, prosecuting attorney, chief witness—all occupying the judicial bench to mete out "impartial" justice to me. This was no less a personage than his Honor, Mayor Walcott, of Columbus, and the kind of "justice" I received from him was that I was ordered sent to jail without a hearing, on $300 bond, the charge being simply that of "disorderly conduct," which was a trumped-up charge to get me behind the bars, and thus preclude the possibility of my speaking in Columbus that night—in other words a foul conspiracy to crush free speech. But suppose the charge of "disorderly conduct" was true? This very Mayor dismisses from his Court every day in the week the worst characters on a small fine.

I remained in jail all night, was well treated by the Sheriff, with the exception that he had a good many "friends" whom he, too, brought up to see me. My attorneys sued out a writ of habeas corpus and brought me before a Judge who refused to grant it, but who reduced my bail from $300 to $100, to stand trial the middle of April on a charge of "disorderly conduct."

I know my communication is rather lengthy, but it is as brief as

I could possibly make it and give the bare, plain facts in this remarkable case of "impartial justice." Let the people of America read and ponder—those of them who believe the laws are administered alike for rich and poor—and in reading I hope they will lose sight of me and see the simple fact that it is not I who am on trial, but free speech—and ask themselves where are their boasted liberties drifting when a petty tyrant of a Mayor can, with impunity, "declare a meeting off" and lock the speaker up on a trumped-up charge. As to the vile libel about my using "obscene language," the thousands of my friends who know me in this and other cities, can bear witness that no language is ever used by me unbecoming a lady.

Letter to the Editor, first published in
the *Columbus Sunday Capital*; and
reprinted in the *Agitator*, March 1887

FOREWORD TO THE
LIFE OF ALBERT R. PARSONS

In preparing the *Life of Albert R. Parsons* for publication I have been actuated by one desire alone, viz.: that I might demonstrate to every one, the most prejudiced as well as the most liberal minds: first, that my husband was no aider, nor abettor, nor counselor of crime in any sense. Second, that he knew nothing of nor had anything to do with the preparation for the Haymarket meeting, and that the Haymarket meeting was intended to be peaceable, and was peaceable until interfered with by the police. Third, that Mr Parsons' connection with the labor movement was purely and simply for the purpose of bettering the condition of his fellow men; that he gave his time, talents, and at last his life, to this cause.

In order to make these facts undeniable, I obtained articles from persons holding avowedly adverse views with his, but who were nevertheless willing to testify to his innocence of the crime for which he suffered death, and his sterling integrity as a man.

It has been the endeavor of the author to make the present work not only biographical, but historical—a work which might be relied upon as an authority by all future writers upon the matters contained in it. Hence nothing has been admitted to its pages that is not absolutely correct, so far as it was possible for me to verify it by close scrutiny of all matter treated.

And for this reason I ask the public to read its pages carefully, for in this way they will become acquainted with the inmost thoughts of one of the noblest characters of which history bears record.

There is one man whose name and life was so intimately interwoven with one of the stirring periods of this country's history that its history could not be written if his name were omitted. That man is General Ulysses S. Grant. His biographers record no act of his life with more praise than the magnanimous manner in which he treated the Rebel General, Lee, when the latter surrendered his sword to him. Suppose Grant had taken the proffered sword and stabbed his antagonist with it? There would have been no word too detestable to have attached to his name.

Albert R. Parsons surrendered his sword to the wild mob of millionaires when he walked into Court and asked for a fair trial by a jury of his peers. Yet the proud State of Illinois murdered him under the guise of "Law and Order"; foully murdered this innocent man. And upon the heart of her then Governor (Oglesby), who completed the atrocity by ratifying the vile conspiracy conducted by the wild howls of the millionaire rabble, by signing the death warrants of men whom he, as a lawyer, knew were innocent, there is not "one damned spot," but five, to "out."

Thus it is that history repeats itself. In this case it was the old, old cry: "Away with them; they preach a strange doctrine! Crucify Them!" But the grand cause for which they perished still lives.

February 22,1889

SOUTHERN LYNCHINGS

Never since the days of the Spartan Helots has history recorded such brutality as has been ever since the war and as is now being perpetrated upon the Negro in the South. How easy for us to go to Russia and drop a tear of sympathy over the persecuted Jew. But a step across Mason's and Dixon's line will bring us upon a scene of horrors before which those of Russia, bad as they are, pale into insignificance! No irresponsible, blood-thirsty mobs prowl over Russian territory, lashing and lynching its citizens. Even the sex which civilization and custom have shielded from rude assaults are treated as brutally as the men.

Women are stripped to the skin in the presence of leering, white-skinned, black-hearted brutes and lashed into insensibility and strangled to death from the limbs of trees. A girl child of fifteen years was lynched recently by these brutal bullies. Where has justice fled? The eloquence of Wendell Phillips is silent now. John Brown's body lies moldering in the grave. But will his spirit lie there moldering, too? Brutes, inhuman monsters —you heartless brutes—you whom nature forms by molding you in it, deceive not yourselves by thinking that another John Brown will not arise.

As one of the speakers so truly said at a meeting of colored citizens held in this city March 27, to protest against the outrages being perpetrated in the South upon peaceful citizens simply because they are Negroes, "The white race furnished us one John Brown; the next must come from our own race." The whites of the South are not only sowing the wind which they will reap in the whirlwind, but the flame which they will reap in the conflagration, as the following utterances at the meeting mentioned above would indicate: "Prepare for the crisis. We have stood this thing long enough. God helps those who help themselves. The crisis is approaching and we must be prepared."

Chicago, *Freedom*, April 1892; excerpts

OMINOUS TIMES

There are some ominous disturbances of special moment in the Labor world. At New Orleans the street-car men are engaged in a desperate struggle, and, according to the capitalistic press, some "rioting" has occurred, the strikers, it is said, having fired on the police. The Granite Cutter's union has been locked out by the bosses' union, who are engaged in an effort to compel the cutters to change the time of signing the yearly contract from January to January instead of, as heretofore, from May to May.

The men claim that this would give the bosses an increased advantage over them, because in January most of the members are idle and would be compelled to make terms that they would not in May. In several mining districts in Idaho and Wyoming there is a general rebellion, and President Harrison has been requested to hold the United States army in readiness to assist the mine-owners in subjugating their wage-slaves. It also seems that the "all-wise" and "all-merciful" God is adding his quota to the sum of human wretchedness, for he is having the "windows of heaven" all thrown open and pouring down floods upon the bowed heads of his most devout worshipers—the Negroes of the South and the farmers of the West—in the most awful devastation and death! What, with floods, famine, lockouts, strikes, and the unemployed millions, can we expect of the near future?

The contemplation of the misery in store for the farming and wage classes next winter is simply appalling! Yet this need not be if the produce of these producers had not, in former years, passed from their hands and gone to fill the elevators of speculating Board of Trade pirates, and the land belonged to actual settlers, and not, as now, to mortgage sharks, and the wages of the wage-earners had remained in their possession, there would always remain wealth enough among the people to tide them over any unforeseen calamity. When will the people see the real cause of all their woe —the private ownership of the means of life?

Chicago, *Freedom*, June, 1892

RUMBLINGS OF THE COMING STORM

What were those rumblings which have been heard in the iron mills of Pennsylvania and mines of Idaho the last few weeks? They are the rumblings of the approaching Social Revolution which will deluge this world before the end of the present century.

What is the world today but a vast hospital ward? The air is filled with groans and lamentations, and every form of suffering is to be seen twitching and turning on beds of poverty. What a spectacle in a world of plenty!

Go through the world and ask each country you come to, "Do peace, plenty, and happiness dwell here?" and from each the same reply will be made: "Pass on; what you seek is not here."

Pause and listen at the borders of each, and the breeze will waft to your ears the same confused echoes of contention, tumult, revolt, and oppression.

How long can this condition of affairs last?

How much longer must the schoolhouse be robbed that the robbers' factory may be filled with the fair roses that bloom at the firesides of poverty and fade in these hells?

How much longer must our sons be made tramps and criminals and our daughters prostitutes, so that a few may riot in luxury?

How long will the few be permitted to sit in exalted places and answer the complaints of the people in short, terse sentences like this: "We possess all rights; you all duties; perform them or we will have you clubbed by our police, hanged by our Sheriffs, and shot by our militia."

Will these surrender their "rights" peaceably? Never! And they who answer that they will are ignoramuses and idiots and have read history to no purpose.

Chicago, *Freedom*, August 1892

THE "SCAB":
A Result of Conditions

Scab is a new word, and like the individual it represents, it is the result of, and is coined from, the conditions of today. We believe in organization among the wealth-producers because it, for a time at least, enables the wage-slave to withstand the encroachments of the capitalists; it disciplines the raw material of the factory; and besides, men and women who are too ignorant or indolent to organize in the unions of their trades are too ignorant to be amenable to the teachings of the science of economies. But the "scab" is here; he is a factor, and is becoming a more important factor with each day's momentum of the capitalistic system.

Analyzed, who is the scab? A poverty-stricken, disheartened wage-slave—no more, no less.

According to very conservative statistics there are constantly from a million to a million and a half of wealth-producers out of employment. What an army from which to manufacture the scab! And this army is ever on the increase. Can the unionist hope to keep his wages at the present maximum standard with this vast army of men and women who possess every essential of life that he does? Whose daily needs are the same as his? Then what is the unionist and the scab to do?

Stop fighting each other and say unanimously and unitedly the wage-system has outgrown its usefulness, if it ever had any, and must go. Trades Unionist and scab, this is the situation which confronts you today. Will you accept it or will you reject it, and thus rivet tighter the chains that bind you?

Chicago, *Freedom,* August, 1892

❄

THE PROPOSED SLAUGHTER

Is it to be another slaughter of innocent working men like the one which took place in Chicago twenty years ago, at the behest of the capitalistic class, who wished to put men out of the way whom they regarded as dangerous to their reign of robbery?

The conspiracy entered into by the Mine Owners' Association of the states of Colorado and Idaho, acting through their tools—the governors of the above-named states—in kidnaping Charles H. Moyer, William D. Haywood and George Pettibone, and spiriting them out of the state of Colorado when the shadows of night had fallen, when no one might witness the conspiracy save the armed conspirators, savors so much of deeds of "dark ages", long, long gone by, that one in reading it in this twentieth century is forced to tap one's self on the forehead and shake one's self, so to speak, to make sure that they are not dreaming!

What, pray, in the face of such an infamy, becomes of the boasted rights of American citizens under its constitution?

If such an outrage had been perpetrated in a foreign country, the American Navy would have been set in motion, and diplomatic relations would have been "strained"; "Teddy"* would be talking loudly about the "rights" of American citizens. But how different all this is when the rights of the American citizen is ruthlessly set aside by the czars of his own country, if he happens to belong to the working class!

There is such a similarity between the present "great dynamite conspiracy" now being staged for action in Idaho, and that conducted by the capitalistic class in the "Anarchists' Trial" in Chicago nearly twenty years ago, that a brief recapitulation is not out of place.

In the present case, as in the former, the Pinkerton lying thug bobs up with his "evidence." Then there are other detectives of less luminous degrees, to be used as supernumeraries in filling out the less important parts of the tragedy. In the present, as in the former case, dynamite bombs have been planted by the "conspirators" and conveniently found by the detectives, and too, like the former case, the "conspiracy" is to date back a few years. This is done to keep the public in breathless expectancy, like the clown in the circus who announces in clarion tones the wonders soon to be brought forth! The governor of Idaho, chief clown just now, begins to talk loudly about "a conspiracy that is going to shock civilization."

This is decidedly *à la mode* Bonfield, Schaack, Grinell, etc. People of America—citizens, brothers and sisters, lovers of liberty and justice—are you going to stand idly by and see these men murdered by the Mine Owners' Association of the states of Idaho and Colorado because they want them out of the way—because they are "troublesome characters"?

If you do not wish to see American soil again stained with the blood of innocent workingmen; if you do not wish to again hear the sound of the accursed gallows as it strangles their voices and forever silences them, then waste not an hour, bestir yourselves! Act now!

Let your voices be heard in protest from the Atlantic to the Pacific, from Maine to Mexico. Serve notice upon the murderous capitalistic class that you will not again stand idly by and see your brothers made victims because they so will it, and they will dare not do it!

Show by your action, your strength and your determination that the people are more powerful than a few rich conspirators.

Chicago, *The Liberator,* March 4, 1905

SUNDAY NITE, NOV 9th.
"Commemorating the Haymarket Riot"
Chairman: DR. BEN REITMAN

Speakers

| Lucy Parsons | George Schilling |
| Nina Spies | John Loughman |

Announcement of a Haymarket Memorial
at the Dil Pickle (early 1930s)

At the Haymarket Martyrs' Monument,
Waldheim (now Forest Home) Cemetery,
Forest Park, Illinois, 1937
(photograph by Arthur Weinberg)

SPEECHES
at the Founding Convention of the
INDUSTRIAL WORKERS OF THE WORLD

Afternoon Session, June 28

A great deal has been said here about the number of votes that the different delegates carry around in their pockets. I am not here for the purpose of raising a note of inharmony or disunion among these delegates. I am simply here in the interest of truth as I see it. Now, this idea of mere force of numbers sounds too much to me like "Might makes Right." Mere force of numbers never made a right on Earth, and, thanks to justice, never can. What is right, what is just and justice, is simply the result of the best minds of all the ages. Whatever right we have in society is simply a heritage handed down to us by those who had only disinterested motives.

Now, I am one of those who entered my name as an individual delegate. I had to do so because I had to subscribe to the technicality of the clause that has been read by the delegate before the last. I entered myself as an individual delegate, but let me assure you that I for one had no such idea of entering my name as an individual delegate. Now a great many of you represent your unions, and I certainly do believe in organized labor or I would not be here; organization of a purely economic nature. I entered my name believing that I did not represent a mere body that met within the four walls of any hall, but that I represent that great body that has its face to the foremost ends of the Earth. Now, I entered my name here, and I think others did, because we had eyes to see the misery, we had ears to hear the cry of the downcast and miserable of the Earth, we had a heart that was sympathetic, and we believed that we could come here and raise our voice and mingle it with yours in the interest of humanity.

So that is the great audience I represent. I represent those people, those little children who, after my twenty-five years' residence in Chicago, I know are in the factories. I entered here as a delegate to represent that great mass of outraged humanity, my sisters whom I can see in the night when I go out in Chicago, who are young and fair and beautiful, but who are compelled to sell the holy name of womanhood for a night's lodging. I am here to raise my voice with them, and ask you to put forth from this organization a declaration of principles and a constitution that shall give them hope in the future, that they shall be enrolled under the banner of this organization.

Had I simply come here to represent myself, I might as well have remained at home and not taken up the time of your deliberative body. Let me say to you—I will take but a few moments of your time—that it matters not to me personally what you shall finally decide. I am perfectly willing to leave my case in the hands of this convention as to whether I and the rest of the individual delegates shall be admitted. I wish simply to say to you, Godspeed you in your effort, and that there might come some good at least from your organization.

I wish to state in conclusion that some of the delegates seem to lay some capital up, or put some stress upon, what some delegate or some people here have lost in the interest of labor. Let me say to you that I think that is the last stock in trade that any delegate should talk about in this hall. It matters not if there is a man in this hall who has lost a limb in the interest of labor—he has not lived in vain. If there are some here who have lost their liberty temporarily in the interest in labor, they have not spent their time in vain. And if there are some who have lost their dearest gift of all, life, in the interest of labor, that cause is justified and their lives have not been sacrificed in vain.

And so let me say to you brothers and sisters, don't engage in any personalities, but simply remember that we are here as one brotherhood and one sisterhood, as one humanity, with a responsibility to the downtrodden and the oppressed of all humanity, it matters not under what flag or in what country they happened to be born. Let us have that idea of Thomas Paine, that "The world is my country, and mankind are my countrymen."

Afternoon Session, June 29

I can assure you that after the intellectual feast that I have enjoyed immensely this afternoon, I feel fortunate to appear before you now in response to your call. I do not wish you to think that I am here to play upon words when I tell you that I stand before you and feel much like a pigmy before intellectual giants, but that is only the fact.

I wish to state to you that I have taken the floor because no other woman has responded, and I feel that it would not be out of place for me to say in my poor way a few words about this movement. We, the women of this country, have no ballot even if we wished to use it, and the only way that we can be represented is to take a man to represent us. You men have made such a mess of it in representing us that we have not much confidence in asking you; and I for one feel very backward in asking the men to represent me. We have no ballot, but we have our labor. I think it is August Bebel, in his *Woman in the Past, Present and Future*—a book that should be read by every woman that works for wages—Bebel says that men have been slaves throughout all the ages, but that woman's condition has been worse, for she has been the slave of a slave.

There was never a greater truth uttered. We are the slaves of the slaves. We are exploited more ruthlessly than men. Wherever wages are to be reduced the capitalist class use women to reduce them, and if there is anything that you men should do in the future it is to organize the women. And I say that if the women had inaugurated a boycott of the State Street stores since the teamsters' strike, the stores would have surrendered long ago. I do not stand before you to brag. I had no man connected with that strike to make it of interest to me to boycott the stores, but I have not bought one penny's worth there since that strike was inaugurated. I intended to boycott all of them as one individual at least, so it is important to educate the women.

Now, I wish to show my sisters here that we fasten the chains of slavery upon our sisters, sometimes unwittingly, when we go down to the department store and look around so cheap. When we come to reflect it simply means the robbery of our sisters, for we know that the things cannot be made for such prices and give women who made them fair wages. I wish to say that I have attended many conventions in the twenty-seven years since I came here to Chicago, a young girl, so full of life and animation and hope. It is to youth that hope comes; it is to age that reflection comes. I have attended conventions from that day to this, of one kind and another, and taken part in them. I have taken part in some in which our Comrade Debs had a part. I was at the organization that he organized in this city some eight or ten years ago. Now, the point I want to make is that these conventions are full of enthusiasm. And that is right; we should sometimes mix sentiment with soberness; it is a part of life.

But when you go out of this hall, when you have laid aside your enthusiasm, then comes the solid work. Are you going out of here with your minds made up that the class which we call ourselves, revolutionary Socialists so-called—that class, is organized to meet organized capital with the millions at its command? It has many weapons to fight us. First, it has money. Then, it has legislative tools. Then, it has armories; and last, it has the gallows. We call ourselves revolutionists. Do you know what the capitalists mean to do to you revolutionists? I simply throw these hints out that you young people may become reflective and know what you have to face at the first, and then it will give you strength. I am not here to cause any discouragement, but simply to encourage you to go on in your grand work.

Now, that is the solid foundation that I hope this organization will be built on; that it may be built not like a house upon the sand, that when the waves of adversity come it may go over into the ocean of oblivion; but that it shall be built upon a strong, granite, hard foundation; a foundation made up of the hearts and aspirations of the men and women of this twentieth century, who have set their minds, their hands, their hearts and their heads against the past with all its miserable poverty, with its wage-slaves, with its children ground into dividends, with its miners away down under the earth and with never the light of sunshine, and with its women selling the holy name of womanhood for a day's board. I hope we understand that this organization has set its face against that iniquity, and that it has set its eyes to the rising star of liberty, that means fraternity, solidarity, the universal brotherhood of man. I hope that while politics have been mentioned here—I am not one of those who, because a man or woman disagrees with me, cannot act with them—I am glad and proud to say I am too broad-minded to say they are a fakir or fool or a fraud because they disagree with me.

My view may be narrow and theirs may be broad; but I do say to those who have intimated politics here as being necessary or a part of this organization, that I do not impute to them dishonesty or impure motives. But as I understand the call for this convention, politics had no place here; it was simply to be an economic organization, and I hope for the good of this organization that when we go away from this hall, and our comrades go some to the west, some to the east, some to the north and some to the south, while some remain in Chicago, and all spread this light over this broad land and carry the message of what this convention has done, that there will be no room for politics at all.

There may be room for politics; I have nothing to say about that; but it is a bread and butter question, an economic issue, upon which the fight must be made. Now, what do we mean when we say revolutionary Socialist? We mean that the land shall belong to the landless, the tools to the toiler, and the products to the producers. Now, let us analyze that for just a moment, before you applaud me. First, the land belongs to the landless. Is there a single land owner in this country who owns his land by the constitutional rights given by the constitution of the United States who will allow you to vote it away from him? I am not such a fool as to believe it. We say, "The tools belong to the toiler." They are owned by the capitalist class. Do you believe they will allow you to go into the halls of the legislature and simply say, "Be it enacted that on and after a certain day the capitalist shall no longer own the tools and the factories and the places of industry, the ships that plow the ocean and our lakes?"

Do you believe that they will submit? I do not. We say, "The product belongs to the producers." It belongs to the capitalist class as their legal property. Do you think that they will allow you to vote them away from them by passing a law and saying, "Be it enacted that on and after a certain day Mr Capitalist shall be dispossessed?" You may, but I do not believe it. Hence, when you roll under your tongue the expression that you are revolutionists, remember what that word means. It means a revolution that shall turn all these things over where they belong—to the wealth producers.

Now, how shall the wealth-producers come into possession of them? I believe that if every man and every woman who works, or who toils in the mines, the mills, the workshops, the fields, the factories and the farms in our broad America should decide in their minds that they shall have that which of right belongs to them, and that no idler shall live upon their toil, and when your new organization, your economic organization, shall declare as man to man and woman to woman, as brothers and sisters, that you are determined that you will possess these things, then there is no army that is large enough to overcome you, for you yourselves constitute the army. Now, when you have decided that you will take possession of these things, there will not need to be one gun fired or one scaffold erected.

You will simply come into your own, by your own independence and your own manhood, and by asserting your own individuality, and not sending any man to any legislature in any State of the American Union to enact a law that you shall have what is your own; yours by nature and by your manhood and by your very presence upon this Earth. Nature has been lavish to her children. She has placed in this Earth all the material of wealth that is necessary to make men and women happy. She has given us brains to go into her storehouse and bring from its recesses all that is necessary. She has given us these two hands and these brains to manufacture them on a parallel with all other civilizations.

There is just one thing we lack, and we have only ourselves to blame if we do not become free. We simply lack the intelligence to take possession of that hope, and I feel that the men and women who constitute a convention like this can come together and organize that intelligence. I feel that you will at least listen to me, and maybe you will disagree with it.

I wish to say that my conception of the future method of taking possession of this Earth is that of the general strike; that is my conception of it. The trouble with all the strikes in the past has been this: the workingmen, like the teamsters of our cities, these hard-working teamsters, strike and go out and starve. Their children starve. Their wives get discouraged. Some feel that they have to go out and beg for relief, and to get a little coal to keep the children warm, or a little bread to keep the wife from starving, or a little something to keep the spark of life in them so that they can remain wage-slaves. That is the way with the strikes in the past.

My conception of the strike of the future is not to strike and go out and starve, but to strike and remain in and take possession of the necessary property of production. If anyone is to starve—I do not say it is necessary—let it be the capitalist class. They have starved us long enough, while they have had wealth and luxury and all that is necessary. You men and women should be imbued with the spirit that is now displayed in far-off Russia and far-off Siberia where we thought the spark of manhood and womanhood had been crushed out of them. Let us take example from them.

We see the capitalist class fortifying themselves today behind their Citizen's Associations and Employers' Associations in order that they may crush the American labor movement. Let us cast our eyes over to far-off Russia and take heart and courage from those who are fighting the battle there, and from the further fact shown in the dispatches that appear this morning in the news that carries the greatest terror to the capitalist class throughout the world—the emblem that has been the terror of all tyrants through all the ages, and there you will see that the red flag has been raised.

According to the *Tribune*, the greatest terror is evinced in Odessa and all through Russia because the red flag has been raised. They know that where the red flag has been raised whoever enroll themselves beneath that flag recognize the universal brotherhood of man; they recognize that the red current that flows through the veins of all humanity is identical, that the ideas of all humanity are identical; that those who raise the red flag, it matters not where, whether on the sunny plains of China, or on the sun-beaten hills of Africa, or on the far-off snow-capped shores of the north, or in Russia or America—that they all belong to the human family and have an identity of interest. That is what they know.

So when we come to decide, let us sink such differences as nationality, religion, politics, and set our eyes eternally and forever towards the rising star of the industrial republic of labor; remembering that we have left the old behind and have set our faces toward the future. There is no power on Earth that can stop men and women who are determined to be free at all hazards. There is no power on Earth so great as the power of intellect. It moves the world and it moves the Earth.

Now, in conclusion, I wish to say to you—and you will excuse me because of what I am going to say and only attribute it to my interest in humanity. I wish to say that nineteen years ago on the fourth of May of this year, I was one of those at a meeting at the Haymarket in this city to protest against eleven workingmen being shot to pieces at a factory in the southeastern part of this city because they had dared to strike for the eight-hour movement that was to be inaugurated in America in 1886.

The Haymarket meeting was called primarily and entirely to protest against the murder of comrades at the McCormick factory. When that meeting was nearing its close someone threw a bomb. No one knows to this day who threw it except the man who threw it. Possibly he has rendered his account with nature and has passed away. But no human being alive knows who threw it. And yet in the soil of Illinois, the soil that gave a Lincoln to America, the soil in which the great, magnificent Lincoln was buried, in the State that was supposed to be the most liberal in the union, five men sleep the last sleep in Waldheim under a monument that has been raised there because they dared to raise their voices for humanity. I say to any of you who are here and can do so, it is well worth your time to go out there and draw some inspiration around the graves of the first martyrs who fell in the great industrial struggle for liberty on American soil.

I say to you that even within the sound of my voice, only two short blocks from where we meet today, the scaffold was erected on which those five men paid the penalty for daring to raise their voices against the iniquities of the age in which we live.

We are assembled here for the same purpose. And do any of you older men remember the telegrams that were sent out from Chicago while our comrades were not yet even cut down from the cruel gallows?

"Anarchy is dead, and these miscreants have been put out of the way."

Oh, friends, I am sorry that I even had to use that word, "anarchy" just now in your presence, which was not in my mind at the outset.

So if any of you wish to go out there and look at this monument that has been raised by those who believed in their comrades' innocence and sincerity, I will ask you, when you have gone out and looked at the monument, that you will go the reverse side of the monument and there on the reverse side the words of a man, himself the purest and the noblest man who ever sat in the gubernatorial chair of the State of Illinois, John P. Altgeld. On that monument you will read the clause of his message in which he pardoned the men who were lingering then in [prison in] Joliet.

I have nothing more to say. I ask you to read the words of Altgeld, who was at that time the governor, and had been a lawyer and a judge, and knew whereof he spoke, and then take out your copybooks and copy the words of Altgeld when he released those who had not been slaughtered at the capitalists' behest, and then take them home and change your minds about what those men were put to death for.

Now, I have taken up your time in this because I simply feel that I have a right as a mother, and as a wife of one of those sacrificed men, to say whatever I can to bring the light to bear upon this conspiracy and to show you the way it was. Now, I thank you for the time that I have taken up of yours. I hope that we will meet again some time, you and I, in some hall where we can meet and organize the wage workers of America, the men and women, so that the children may not go into the factories, nor the women into the factories, unless they go under proper conditions.

I hope even now to live to see the day when the first dawn of the new era will have arisen, when capitalism will be a thing of the past, and the new industrial republic, the commonwealth of labor, shall be in operation. I thank you.

Proceedings of the Founding Convention of the IWW, 1905

OUR LABEL: THE IWW LABEL

The *Liberator* is issued under the label of the Industrial Workers of the World. We considered for some time whether or not we should put on the label of the Allied Printing Trades Council or the Industrial Workers of the World. We finally thought [that] to be consistent, we must use the latter, because the editor of *The Liberator* was a delegate to the [IWW's founding] convention and gave what assistance we were capable of rendering to the formation of the IWW. Besides, we feel confident that the trades union movement has arrived at the parting of the ways. The old will fall back, the new will go forward.

Chicago, The Liberator, September 3, 1905

ARE CLASS INTERESTS IDENTICAL?
A Synopsis of the Aims and Objects of the Industrial Workers of the World

If there is a country on the face of the Earth where the working classes need to be educated to understand their class interests, that country is America. The wage-earners are taught that in this country where every man's son may aspire to become president of these United States, there can be no classes. Large masses accept this kind of "jollying" without question. Thousands of them do really believe we have no classes here. Because one man in thirteen or fourteen million men is elected, instead of being born to rule, they accept this as indisputable evidence of universal liberty.

Another hard fact that is difficult to drive home to the American mind, is that he belongs to an entirely different class from that to which the employing class belongs. Because he sees some of the wage class occasionally escape from the wage to the middle class, he thinks maybe he can do so too; thus he bribes himself to keep quiet, while wrong and oppression are seen on every hand. If he joins his union, it is as a sort of temporary makeshift, or convenience, as he expects to become a businessman, or learn a profession or his son will be a professional or businessman, or his daughter will marry a rich man or something of the kind will happen; so he goes on from year to year, bribing himself; meanwhile his condition and that of his class become more and more hopeless.

Then too, the teachings of the trades unions are based upon wrong premises, in so far as they teach the "identity of interests between capital and labor." If the interests of capital and labor are identical, why do they not both belong to the same organization? We need to view from the right standpoint the class struggle; hence when an organization is founded for the express purpose of teaching the working class correct and fundamental principles underlying the wage-system and their own relation to the employing class, and when we understand these lessons are to be taught in the meetings of the unions, then indeed may we hail such an organization as a real blessing!

The Industrial Workers of the World was launched in Chicago, July 8th, 1905 with the avowed purpose of demonstrating that, "the working class and the employing class have nothing in common." That the readers of *The Liberator* may understand what the Industrial Workers of the World really stand for, we give the Preamble of the Constitution:

IWW PREAMBLE

The working class and the employing class have nothing in common. There can be no peace so long as hunger and want are found among the millions of working people, and the few, who make up the employing class, have all the good things of life. Between these two classes a struggle must go on until all the toilers come together on the political, as well as on the industrial field, and take and hold that which they produce by their labor through an economic organization of the working class without affiliation with any political party. The rapid gathering of wealth and centering of the management of the industries into fewer and fewer hands make the trades unions unable to cope with the ever-growing power of the employing class, because the trades unions foster a state of things which allows one set of workers to be pitted against another set of workers in the same industry, thereby helping to defeat one another in wage wars. The trades unions aid the employing class to mislead the workers into the belief that the working class have interests in common with their employers. These sad conditions can be changed and the interests of the working class upheld only by an organization formed in such a way that all its members in any one industry, or in all industries, if necessary, cease work whenever a strike or a lockout is on in any department thereof, thus making an injury to one, an injury to all.

Chicago, *The Liberator,* September 3, 1905

SALUTATION
to the Friends of Liberty

In this age of quick transmission of thought, when all our energies are strained to learn more and more about the sayings and doings of our fellow beings, and especially those who are engaged in the same line of work with ourselves, it becomes absolutely necessary for us to have a medium of exchange if we are to keep in touch with each other, and if we are to do any effective work. I believe we have all felt this need most intensely since the suspension of *Free Society.*

The Liberator comes to fill this want.

Comrades, are you ready to support the paper? Are you ready to give your moral and financial assistance?

If the paper is not what you wish it to be, then make it so, write articles, send in reports about meetings and reform movements generally in your vicinity. The paper is yours, make of it what you choose.

Articles will be published from comrades and friends with the thanks of the editor.

The line will be drawn sharply at personalities as we know these enlighten no one and do infinitely more harm than good.

The editor has been too busy getting out the paper upon the date promised to correspond with many writers of known ability requesting them to contribute to *The Liberator*, but will do so very soon.

Among those who have been written to and have promised to contribute articles are the well-known historian and scholar C. L. James,* who will contribute a series of articles on "Anarchism Defined." The first one appears in this issue.

These articles will begin in the simplest form and lead the reader gradually, step by step into the philosophy of anarchism. Al Klemencic, of Pueblo, Col., will keep our readers posted upon the labor movement in the middle west. Albert Ryan, whose style and energy is here given us under head of "correspondence," and who is a member of the Western Federation of Miners, will keep us posted on everything of interest in his part of the world. We will endeavor to find some one on the Pacific coast to keep us informed from that part of the country. E. N. Ling has promised us a series of articles, beginning in October, showing the condition of the farming class. As Mr Ling is a farmer and has been engaged in agricultural pursuits both in this country and Canada we may expect something from his pen that will be interesting and practical. And, too, our readers will become quite familiar with the facile pen of "Rex."

Hoping comrades will overlook the defects and shortcomings of the management of this paper, remembering that the editor lays no claim to being a trained writer, and where mistakes occur, they will be mistakes of the head and not of the heart.

Salutations and greetings to all friends of Liberty, Solidarity and Equality.

Chicago, The Liberator, Sept. 3, 1905

ON REVOLUTION IN RUSSIA AND THE CHINESE USE OF THE BOYCOTT

What has ever been granted to the countless millions of workers of Earth without a fight? Czar Nicholas has discovered that he is not all Russia. Will he "let the voice of the people be heard"? Was it argument or force that changed Czar Nicholas's mind? Well, the Russian people have gotten the thin edge of the wedge in; let them keep striking hard, they will split the throne after a while.

How do you like the land grab of 2,000,000 men fighting in Manchuria for their bosses? How many of these 2,000,000 will profit by it?

How many inventors to your knowledge have profited by their inventions? But how many inventors have helped to enrich the capitalist?

If all genius and ability were diverted toward the good of humanity at large, what a vast number of half-starved overworked men, women and children would be taking a much needed vacation!

In the "good old days" when about the only information that we, God's anointed, were enabled to obtain from heathen lands came by way of the missionaries, we were led in our guileless innocence to believe that the only use we good Christians could possibly have for the "benighted heathen" was to set his feet upon the straight and narrow path that leads to heaven (*our* heaven).

But, lo and behold! Our "captains of industry," ever with an eye to business and affairs of this world, discovered that the heathen had backs to cover as well as souls to save, so it came to pass that the good Christians' shoddy goods were pressed, fairly forced upon said heathen. But the heathen must be content, he must not assume for one moment that he is desirable company for Christians to associate with. But right here, the whole beautifully arranged plan of our capitalists seems likely to come to a bad end, so the whole governmental machinery at Washington—"Teddy" to boot—is set in motion to save the commercial pirates who it seems are not practicing what they preach. They are not putting their "faith in God," but are calling lustily upon the government to save them!

Right here is where the tricks of the "heathen" Chinese are playing havoc. The Chinaman has reasoned it out (if a "heathen" can reason), that if his money is good enough to fill the pockets of Christians, why should he be excluded from their country? The Chinaman has failed to adopt the Christians' religion. He has nevertheless found his weapon, the boycott—a very powerful and effective instrument indeed. He is answering the Exclusion Act by using it—hence the wailing and gnashing of teeth in the Christians' camp.

But the Chinaman is very complacent. He has formed a kind of union, which refuses to let ships discharge their cargoes. The Chinaman knows that he got along in his own country for countless centuries. Contented in his own way, he never went to convert anyone to his way of thinking; if strangers came within his gates of their own free will and cared to investigate his religion and philosophy, well and good; if not, it was all the same. What the Chinaman wished above all else was to be let alone.

The Liberator, September 3, 1905;
excerpts from "Every Day Reflections"

INDUSTRIAL EVOLUTION & LABOR DAY:
The AFL versus the IWW

As the Knights of Labor went down, the American Federation of Labor commenced to rise.

This latter organization, after about twenty-three years' existence, claims over a million members. It was the AFL that inaugurated "Labor Day," the first Monday in September. This Labor Day was originally intended to be the one day in the year on which labor could devote to its own interests, for the purpose of cultivating a spirit of solidarity and fraternity among the working class. But "Labor Day" has lost this feature—instead, it has degenerated into a day when politicians, fakers and grafters have full swing, and a free platform to lie, and to gull the masses.

All the evidences of disintegration are apparent in the AFL at the present time. One does not have to be an enemy to make this statement; in fact, the writer is a friend to organized labor, but facts are facts, nevertheless. The American Federation of Labor is doomed: first, because of its own inherent rottenness; and second, because, in common with all other craft organizations, it has outgrown its usefulness, and must give way to the next step in evolution, which is the Industrial Union, which proposes to organize along industrial lines, the same as capital is organized.

While I am positive the days of the AFL are numbered, I nevertheless recognize and am compelled to give credit to that organization for the great benefit it has been to the working classes of America.

On the ruins of the AFL, there is at the present moment arising the Industrial Union which was organized in Chicago, July 8th, 1905. This industrial organization is organized along the lines of Industrial Evolution, hence it is bound to succeed.

A reply to a reader's inquiry,
The Liberator, September 5, 1905

WOMAN:
Her Evolutionary Development

In the earlier times of the world's history when man was but little higher in the intellectual scale than the beast which he slew for food, and whose skins he used for raiment, muscular strength and physical endurance were the standards of excellence and the stamp of superiority which prevailed. As nature had not endowed woman with these requisites to the same extent she had man, he looked upon her as a being inferior to himself. Possibly this was the beginning of man's domination and woman's subjugation. But as man ascended in the social scale of development, he began to acquire property, which he wished to transmit along with his name to his offspring—then woman became his household drudge.

She was regarded as a sort of necessary evil; as something to be used and abused; to be bought and sold—as a thing fit only to cater to his pleasures and his passions—this was woman's lowly position. For countless centuries, the drudge went her lonesome, weary way, bore the children—and man's abuse—but the long sweep of the centuries was to bring relief at last! When the steam engine was harnessed and placed in the field of production, muscles were practically eliminated as a factor in producing the world's wealth. This enabled woman to leave the narrow confines of the kitchen where she had been kept for so long.

She entered the arena of life's activities, to make her way in this hustling, pushing, busy world as an independent human being for the first time in the world's history. Oh, the direful predictions that were made if woman dared leave home to work! Why, she would become coarse, mannish, unsexed, etc.—but all to no purpose; woman went, she saw and conquered! Woman rapped long, loud and waited patiently at the college door before it was grudgingly opened to her.

"What," exclaimed conventionality, "Our daughters go in the dissecting room with men? Never!"

But stern progress brushed aside all these objections. Experience has taught that woman can study "the human form divine" by the side of her brothers and lose not one whit of her womanly charms or modesty. Now parents are just as proud to witness their daughters receiving diplomas as they are their sons. I know of no activity from which woman is debarred because of her sex. Who will claim the change has not benefitted all humanity? But woman is allowing herself to be used to reduce the standard of life by working for lower wages than those demanded by men; this she will have to rectify, else her labor will become a detriment instead of a blessing or a help either to herself or her fellow workers.

Chicago, *The Liberator*, September 10, 1905

THE FACTORY CHILD

Afrer reading a recent census report showing that children (white children) are toiling in the cotton factories of the South for $1.75 per week, one is constrained to inquire: Where do the burdens of capitalism press heaviest? When we see the father who has kissed his loving wife and helpless little ones an affectionate "God bless you" and turn heavily upon his heel to seek employment, he knows not where, that he may furnish them bread, he knows not how much, we are tempted to say of this man that pleasure has become to him a mockery, and misery a part of his being.

When we witness day by day the tired maiden wearing away her young life amid the dismal din of the factory wheels, we may say, here, indeed, the system of wage-slavery must press heaviest. Yet it is not so, for the deep, dark, damnable oppressions of capitalism are felt more keenly by the young and innocent, than by the more mature in years. While some whirl through the short space which time has allotted to them here, and in one grand round of pleasure fairly dance down to their graves as it were unaware, there is a great class who cannot even say their life has been sad from the cradle to the grave, since they never experienced that luxury of childhood's innocence, a cradle; and as to a grave, why the dissecting table is quite good enough for "paupers."

When giddy laughter and wine-bibbed mirth rings out from within the soft silken-hung halls and finds its way through gilded casements and echoes along down the broad avenues of ease, it here encounters a counter echo—this last proceeding from some noisome, dark, forbidding alley where dwell the weary little toilers, where "balmy sleep" refuses to light on lids so flooded with hot, burning tears—this last echo in the wail of the factory child, whose twitching nerves, and aching limbs refuse to be calmed after the long strain of the day's drudgery. It is here, indeed, that the climax of misery and oppression has been reached.

It is the slaughtering of the innocents. It is the coining of these little ones into precious diadems to deck "my lady's brow," that brow which was never sullied by care or want. Yet why cannot this be said of the factory child, the producer of so much wealth? O

94

factory child, what sage has sung thy song correct? Who thy tale of misery hath half told? What tongue or pen has yet been found powerful enough to depict thy wrongs in words that could touch the callous heart, that sacrifices thy innocence to the lust of greed!

O factory child! What can be said of thee, thou wee, wan thing? 'Tis thy teardrop which flashes from the jeweled hand of the factory lord. 'Tis thy blood which colors the rubies worn in his gorgeous drawing room.

But those tears of thy young years shall not be shed in vain; thy blood will not always be crystallized on the fingers of dainty ladies. O, child of late! Have patience amid the murmurs of discontent, which will be wafted back to you on every breeze that kisses thy pale cheek in the struggle of the coming years.

Toil on, toil on, thou victim of capitalism! Some day thy tears will be dried; some day thy chest will cease to heave. For brave hearts and strong arms will annihilate the accursed system which binds you down to drudgery and death. Only then will the factory door to tender childhood be forever closed, and the schoolhouse be flung open, and all the avenues of art and learning be opened up to children of the producing many.

Men! Producers of the world's wealth, press on to the front! Unfurl the banner of revolution, fling it to the breeze, and let its folds stream out to catch the incoming breeze which whispers liberty, fraternity, equality.

Rescue your little ones from the deep, dark, damnable throes of capitalism. Be men! Dare and do.

Chicago, The Liberator, September 10, 1905

THE BALLOT HUMBUG

Whatever we hear from all quarters we are very apt to believe, whether it requires some effort to believe, whether it is true or not, especially if it requires some effort to examine it. Of all the modern delusions, the ballot has certainly been the greatest. Yet most of the people believe in it.

In the first place, it is founded on the principle that the *majority shall lead* and the minority *must follow* (no matter whether it will be any advantage to the majority to have the minority follow them or not). Let us take a body of legislators, absolutely honest, and see what they can do. A, B and C have each a distinct principle to carry out, and there is no good reason why each one should not carry out his principle to a certain extent without interfering with the other two. Politics steps in and says: let us decide this matter by the ballot, for that is fair. What is the result? A and C finally reach a compromise and unite by giving up a portion of their ideas. A and C are then the majority and B's principles get no further consideration, but are simply ruled out of existence. This is majority *rule*.

Notice the result. Instead of three well-defined principles that might have been continued, developed and enjoyed, we have lost one altogether, and corrupted the other two. This is the inevitable result of majority rule in a legislative body which attempts to manufacture laws to enforce upon people of large communities who have all kinds of conflicting interests.

Of course it is better to have majority rule if it represents the real wishes of a large number of people than to have minority rule which is only in the interest of the few, as is the case today, where all laws are practically in the interest of the capitalistic class. But the principle of rulership is in itself wrong; no man has any right to rule another man.

Of course, if one is invading the rights of another, he must be restrained. This is not rulership, but self-preservation. Let us see for example, how our law factories are operated. A corruptionist works a majority as follows: He hires a tool called an attorney or lobbyist to hang around the capitol and buttonhole the members of the legislature and present to them his scheme in the brightest colors and in a way that will make it appear to be a great blessing to the country. In this way, together with some graft, he usually gets the votes of the majority of the members.

If the scheme to be put through is so barefaced that the majority cannot be misled into voting for it, then the job is done by a compromise. The lobbyist has persuaded A that the bill is all right, and B, being opposed to it—but favoring some other scheme that A opposes—it is only necessary to get B to agree to vote for the bill on condition that A will vote for B's bill when it comes up. This scheme is called honest, or at least "all things are fair in politics." The lobbyist who is running A might have put the two jobs up with the lobbyist who was running B.

Thus do our lobbyists use one member of the legislative bodies against another to pry a fat job out of the people for the benefit of the moneybags. It makes no difference who the member of congress may be, or what his principles may be—the job can be worked on him just the same. Therefore, what does the people's voting amount to in the choice of members?

Let us take this example: Suppose a legislature is composed of ninety-nine members; on the above scheme, twenty-five will make a majority, even if all are present; the twenty-five swap jobs with twenty-five more and thus make fifty votes—a majority of *one*. The lobbyist makes it his business to know how many are sick or absent, or he strives to bet the worst opponents on commissions or investigating committees out of town. But there is much in trading votes, for each member generally feels like keeping his trades to himself, or can be persuaded to do so, therefore it is easy to trade A's vote with B, C, D and E and make each one think that he alone traded with A. In this way ten such men as A can easily get four a majority of ninety-nine, and ten such men are not hard to find when capital has use for them.

But this is not the end. A cannot trade with F, so A introduces a bill or an amendment repulsive to F and then agrees to drop it on condition that F will either vote for the bill or be absent when it comes up. These are some of the tricks played in law-making.

Can you blame an Anarchist who declares that man-made laws are not sacred? Society would not disband or revert to barbarism if laws were done away with. With thousands of laws being enacted and hundreds of corruptionists playing their tricks, what becomes of the voter's victory at the polls? What becomes of his reforming all things by the use of the ballot? So long as he is willing to submit to a bad law until it is repealed, what better leverage do rogues want on humanity?

The fact is *money* and *not* votes is what rules the people. And the capitalists no longer care to buy the voters, they simply buy the "servants" after they have been elected to "serve." The idea that the poor man's vote amounts to anything is the veriest delusion. The ballot is only the paper veil that hides the tricks.

Can you blame an Anarchist when he sees a political bummer conniving for a job in a law factory that he fails to see anything sacred about him, or his laws? We know there never was a law passed that ever prevented one single crime from being committed. We know crime will cease only when men are taught to do good, because it makes them happier to do right than wrong. We know that if passing laws would have prevented crime or made men better, that we would all be angels by now.

We say: Turn the law factories into schools and place scientists in them to teach the truths of human solidarity, love and fraternity, and make these possible by abolishing monopoly in the means of life, and mankind will quickly develop that which is best, noblest and purest in his nature.

Chicago, *The Liberator*, September 10, 1905

WAGE-SLAVES *VS.* CORPORATIONS:
What Are You Going to Do About It?

It has not been so many years ago since it was an accepted fact that this was a middle-class Republic. Hence it was immune against those upheavals that have in times past disturbed the equanimity of the "better classes" of Europe. If there are any such persons at the present time hugging these delusions we would be pleased to have them peruse the following extracts, taken from an interview with James R. Keene, of Wall Street fame. He says:

> It is my firm conviction that the day is coming when the individual small merchant will cease to exist. In his place will be millions of persons working for wages and salaries whereas yesterday and today there were and are proprietors. In other words, I believe the time is coming when practically all mercantile and industrial affairs will be conducted by corporations.

Now, Americans, what are you going to do about this evil wave that is rushing in upon you and yours like an inundating flood? Are you going to stand still until it carries you off into the ocean of wage-slavery? Are there not enough there already struggling for a wretched existence?

Oh, I think I hear you say, "Why, I am going to use the ballot, the freeman's weapon, and elect good men to office, who will seize the boa constrictor-like trusts and control them. Are we not free-born American citizens?"

Oh, are you, though? Not too much assurance, please. Let us see what Alton B. Parker* has to say. When asked to comment on the admission of George W. Perkins, vice-president of the New York Life Insurance Company, that Mr McCall had contributed $50,000 of the funds of the company to the Republican campaign fund last year, Mr. Parker said:

Yes, I believe I ought to say, now that there is no political excitement to distract the public attention, that the president of the New York Life was not the only such contributor. The officers of other great life insurance companies, such as the Equitable and the Mutual, also contributed from the policy-holders' funds for campaign purposes last year. What has been proved in the case of the New York Life undoubtedly would be proved in the other cases. Were there an investigation of railroad, manufacturing and other corporations, it would be found that these life insurance officers were not the only corporation officers who put their hands into the treasury and took out moneys belonging to widows and orphans to help secure a partisan triumph.

That their acts were unlawful and their purposes corrupt goes without saying. Such men desire the triumph of that party which will better serve their personal financial interests and will—for contributions, past, present and future—continue to protect those interests by lenient legislation and by pretense at execution of law which shall be tenderly blind to all their offenses. That party they espouse in the boardroom, and contribute to it of the moneys they hold in trust, and, occasionally, a little of their own. . . .

The officers responsible for these raids upon the treasuries of corporations have received their reward in unfettered management of life insurance corporations; in unembarrassed raids upon the public through trusts—condemned by both common and statute law; in refusal to punish criminally the officers of railroad and other corporations violating the laws, and in statutory permission to manufacturing corporations to levy tribute on the people.

There can be no hope of checking the unlawful aggressions of officers of great corporations so long as they may thus form a quasi-partnership with the organization for the dominant political party. For, in the hour when the administration official seeks to punish the offender he is reminded by the head of the organization of the magnitude of the contributions of the corporation.

There is, however, something worse, if possible, than the escape of such offenders from justice. It is the gradual demoralization of voters and the dulling of the public conscience caused by the efforts to make these vast sums of money procure the ballots they were intended to procure, corruptly and otherwise.

Reader, have you read the above carefully? Yes? Then we ask you again: What are you going to do about it? Forty years ago a wail came up from the Sunny South that 4,000,000 black slaves were held in bondage. The eloquent Wendell Phillips, William Lloyd Garrison and many others depicted the auction block, the wail of innocent childhood, the anguish of womanhood who were compelled to do their master's bidding. It is not quite so bad in the North today, it is true, but how many of the wage class, as a class, are there who can avoid obeying the commands of the master (employing) class, as a class? Not many, are there?

Then are you not slaves to the money power as much as were the black slaves to the Southern slaveholders? Then we ask you again: What are you going to do about it? You had the ballot then. Could you have voted away black slavery? You know you could not because the slaveholders would not hear of such a thing for the same reason you can't vote yourselves out of wage-slavery.

The trusts will not allow you to vote them out of power because they *are* the power, as is shown by the interview given above.

All that the master class care for is to rush their "hands" through the factory grist, get all there is of strength and vitality out of them to pay interest on their watered stock, and when they are practically exhausted, then turn them over to the tender mercies of their police, to be "run in" as vagrants.

This is the fate which awaits many of the middle class and the wage-class. What are you going to do about it? Are you going to serve notice on these thieves, and highway robbers, sitting in high places of "honor" and "trust," that by the eternal god of justice, and by the manhood in you, that you will not, in this land of plenty, allow your children to become the mere hirelings and dependents upon the sweet will of their children?

Remind them that the sword still hangs upon the wall and the heart still beats within the man, and that *that* sword will be unsheathed again, if necessary, in defense of your rights. Give them to understand that you will not stand patiently by and see your hard earnings squandered by a luxuriating class of idlers. If the American manhood will arouse itself and speak to those fellows in plain language, not to be misunderstood, they can save themselves, their country and their children, from the fate of poverty which awaits them.

Will you do it?

Chicago, *The Liberator*, September 24, 1905; excerpts; originally titled "Americans! Arouse Yourselves!"

THE WOMAN QUESTION AGAIN?

K*ewanee, Ill., Oct. 2. The funeral of the victims of the tragedy of the Markham home Saturday, in which eight lives were taken by the mother's insane act, was held today. Only two coffins were used, one for Mrs Markham and the other for the seven children she killed, whose charred bodies were taken from the ashes of the home.*

Who can tell the amount of pent-up woe the above brief telegram contains? Here was a young woman of thirty-five years who had given birth to seven children, the eldest one eleven years, the youngest four months old. There was no "race suicide" in that house. The father, we are informed, was a poor truck-farmer in summer and did odd jobs in winter for an existence. The father, on learning of the awful deed, committed suicide on the spot! So the entire family of eight are gone. The first dispatches inform us that Mrs Markham had become despondent over family cares and the loneliness of farm life.

How many more Mrs Markham's are there in America today? This would make interesting statistics if it were possible to gather them. How many of those children would have been born, if the mother's desires had at all times been consulted and respected, is another very interesting question. We dare say not all the seven, for if they had all been welcome children, the mother's heart would never have become so unnatural as to have directed the hand against their lives.

Poor burden-bearing, poverty stricken, care-worn, child-bearing-to-excess Mary Markham, you are gone! And you have taken your sorrows and your little ones with you into the Great Unknown, but you were a victim of our false society which makes it a crime to impart information that would have made your young life a mother's joy, with a few healthy children to caress you; but, instead, you saw from day to day a helpless burden of poverty and despair. Or maybe our care-worn sister was one of those who had been taught, "Wives, submit yourselves unto your husband and his desires at all times."

Let us rejoice that this species of woman is becoming scarcer every day. Let us trust that she will soon become extinct; then we shall have fewer children, better-bred children, and fewer slaves for our factory lords.

Wife Quits Home for "Business"

Here is a very different type of a woman from Mrs Markham. Traveling salesman for a wholesale grocery house was a position more to the liking of Mrs Kate Fitzgibbon Hamblin than that of acting as wife and mother, according to the bill for divorce filed yesterday by Eugene L. Hamblin, president of the Hamblin Printing Company on Dearborn Street. The complainant declares his wife left him and their two children, 7 and 5 years old, to enter the employment of Sprague, Warner & Co., saying she "would rather be a successful businesswoman than a good housekeeper." Mr Hamblin says he even now is willing to take her back.

Probably Mrs Hamblin never intended to sink her whole individuality when she married; finding it impossible not to do so and remain with her husband, she simply left him. Of course she has not deserted her children. What mother ever does? The children will be better raised and cared for with the mother and father separated, if they could not agree, than to be brought up amid an eternal jangle at home between the parents. We assume that Mrs Hamblin is a very estimable woman from the fact that "Mr Hamblin says he even now is willing to take her back."

The "new woman" has made her bow upon the stage of life's activities as an independent human being, and she feels her importance; she feels very different from her man-tagged sisters of passed generations, who imagined they couldn't move without man's assistance.

The sooner men learn to make companions and equals of their wives and not subordinates, the sooner the marriage relation will be one of harmony.

Chicago, *The Liberator,* October 3, 1905

WHAT FREEDOM MEANS

The change from the present method of obtaining one's living is inevitable, because it has become a necessity. We now live under the pay system, in which if you can't pay you can't have. Everything has a price set upon it; earth, air, light and water, all have their price. And he who hasn't worked, let him starve. Love, honor, fame, ambition, all the noblest and holiest aspirations and sentiments of humanity are bought and sold. Everything is upon the market for sale; all is merchandise and commerce. Land, the prime necessity of existence, is held for a price, and the homeless millions perish because they cannot pay for it. Food, raiment and shelter exist in super-abundance, but are withheld for the price.

The productive and distributive forces of nature, united with the power and ingenuity of man are reserved for a price. And humanity perishes from disease, crime and ignorance because of its enforced, artificial poverty. The mental, moral, intellectual and physical qualities are dwarfed, stunted and crushed to maintain the price. This is slavery, the enslavement of man to his own powers: Can it continue? The change is inevitable because necessary. Free access to all the productive and distributive forces will alone free the minds and bodies of men. There are certain things that are priceless. Among these are life, liberty and happiness, and these are the things which the society of the future, the free society, will guarantee to all for the return of a few hours labor per day.

When labor is no longer for sale, society will produce free men and women, who will think free, act free, and be free. Crime and criminals will flee from such a society, because the incentive for crime will be gone.

Chicago, The Liberator, October 8, 1905

FAMOUS WOMEN OF HISTORY

Under the above head will be continued for a few weeks brief sketches of the lives of women who have contributed their share in building the world's history. While the editor will contribute a number of these sketches we also invite others, especially women, to send in brief sketches of famous women, if any such occur to their minds. Let these sketches be well stated, short and to the point. We hope if any are sent in that they will be far superior to those which we write ourselves.

Chicago, The Liberator, February 22, 1905

FAMOUS WOMEN OF HISTORY:
Florence Nightingale

If our social arrangements were so adjusted that each person could follow that calling in life which they are by nature adapted for, what a great gainer society as a whole would be. These few who are so fortunate as to be able to follow the calling of their heart's desire make a success of life. Florence Nightingale was one of the fortunate few, who could engage in that occupation for which she was best adapted. Florence Nightingale was a born nurse. In her was found that rare combination of heart, brain and sympathy which makes the ideal nurse. It is when one is laid low by the ravages of disease that they can appreciate to its utmost depth the value of human kindness.

Many charming stories are told of Florence's sympathetic nature even in her childhood: how she sought out wounded animals, and tenderly nursed them, and how she would scientifically bandage her dolls and would work earnestly at this occupation for hours at a time. Florence Nightingale's parents were of the well-to-do class. Still she was not contented to sit down and live a life of idleness and ease, as so many do who belong to that class. In early womanhood she took an apprenticeship of nine years in different hospitals. This course of training amply equipped her for the arduous labor she was to perform among the wounded from battlefields.

During the Crimean war, Wm. H. Russell wrote a number of letters from the Crimea to the *London Times*. In these letters he demonstrated so clearly that the unsanitary condition of the British army was killing off more men than the deadly battles of the Crimea, that England became panic-stricken over the mortality list, yet seemed helpless to curtail it. In the hurry and enthusiasm at the outbreak of the Crimean war (1854) Great Britain had dispatched shiploads of men improperly provided with food or clothing for the severe Russian climate. Starvation, cholera and agonizing suffering were the results.

Amid the general consternation, the minister of war wrote a letter to Miss Nightingale, stating that he considered her the only person in Great Britain capable of bringing order out of confusion, and imploring her to organize and direct the reform of the military hospitals; and this letter was crossed by one from Miss Nightingale, volunteering to place her strength and ability at the service of her nation. Good trained nurses were almost unknown quantities in those days; yet, nothing daunted, Florence Nightingale sailed from England with thirty of the best nurses that she could muster within a week from her letter. It required a good deal of tact to overcome the prejudices and jealousies among the physicians and surgeons at the "womanly prominence" and to conciliate the general disapproval of medical and military officials. For these were the days when it was considered that "the proper place for woman is at home."

Overcoming professional jealousy, she set herself to the task of cleansing the Augean hospitals containing over 4,000 patients. These barrack hospitals at Scutari, which had been loaned to the British government by the Sultan of Turkey, were 100 feet above the Bosporus. The day before the arrival of the staff of nurses the wounded from Balaclava had been landed; packed in the over-crowded transports, their wounds had not been dressed for five days, and cholera and fever were reaping their fearful harvest. The poor men outside with cold and starvation were faring far better than the sufferers in the tainted wards of the disordered hospitals.

After comparative comfort had been established, Florence Nightingale opened a diet kitchen, where specialties were prepared for the 800 men who could not eat ordinary food; a laundry where, for the first time since they had been brought down from the Crimea, the ragged clothes of the soldiers were washed, and a combination library and schoolroom, where the chaplain aided her in instituting games and lectures for the convalescents.

The most difficult of all the provinces was of course that of nursing, yet it is said that wherever there was the greatest danger of distress, there the faithful head was to be found silently superin-tending, never allowing a severe case to escape her personal treat-ment. To accomplish this she often stood twenty hours at a time, and after the doctors had retired she was to be seen making her nightly rounds through miles of suffering patients, shading with her hand the lamp that she carried, that it might not disturb the sick, many of whom as she passed kissed her shadow on their pillows with passionate enthusiasm. Longfellow has commemorated this incident in his exquisite "Santa Filomena" with such sympathetic touch that no biographer of Florence Nightingale can refrain from quoting it:

> *Lo! in that house of misery*
> *A lady with a lamp I see*
> *Pass through the glimmering gloom,*
> *And flit from room to room.*
> *And slow, as in a dream of bliss,*
> *The speechless sufferer turns to kiss*
> *Her shadow as it falls*
> *Upon the darkening walls.*
> *On England's annals, through the long*
> *Hereafter of her speech and song,*

A light its rays shall cast
From portals of the past.
"A lady with a lamp shall stand
in the great history of the land,
A noble type of good,
Heroic womanhood."

In the future, when the war drum will be heard no more, and the only reveille to be sounded will be that which shall call men to the peaceful walks of life, the name of Florence Nightingale will be revered, as a woman who, though delicate and far removed from want, nevertheless was willing to risk her own life, that she might bring relief to that most stupid victim of our present system, the soldier.

Chicago, *The Liberator,* October 22, 1905

FAMOUS WOMEN OF HISTORY:
Louise Michel

How many are there of the countless millions who have entered this life, passed through its changing scenes and at last have laid down to rest, of whom it can be truly said, "Here rest they who have labored for the uplifting of the oppressed, who have devoted their energies unstintingly in the interest of the 'common people?'" We fear there are few indeed. A life devoted to the interest of the working class; a life of self-abnegation, a life full of love, kindness, gentleness, tragedy, activity, sadness and kind-ness, are some of the characteristics which went to make up the varied life of our comrade, Louise Michel. In the elderly woman, clad in simple black garments, with gray hair curling upon rounded shoulders and kindest of blue eyes glancing from the strongly marked face, none but those who knew her personally would in the last few years have recognized Louise Michel.

Listening to her quiet musical voice, with its slightly rising and falling cadences, uttering sentences which were as dignified and impressive as the lines from a heroic play, it needed some personal knowledge to imagine her calling in the streets of Paris three and thirty years ago to comrades to rally, and encouraging them to stand and defend the street barricades amid the hail of shell and fire.

Still more incredible must the stormy scenes of her long life have seemed to those who only saw her in the little home she only a few years ago found in a London suburb, feeding or caressing the numerous furred and feathered friends housed by her tender charity, many of them bearing the scars of cruelties from which she had tried to save them. For herself she thought nothing of privation and suffering, but for all creation that groans and travails in pain she felt with every nerve and fiber of her mind.

As a girl, while living in the old chateau near Troyes, where she was born, she noticed and questioned the sufferings of the animals that man had subjected. An early novel of hers opens with a graphic description of the sufferings of a worn-out horse which was driven into a pond to feed the leeches bred for Paris doctors. As soon as she could reason, Louise Michel conceived the idea that the world only needed to be taught better to do better. Her ambition was to help in the teaching of it, and she became a schoolmistress. She was teaching school when the troubles of the Franco-Prussian war began; all those years she had been using her pen on political questions, modeling her verse on poems of Victor Hugo, and had already won some reputation among advanced political parties.

When it was proposed to surrender Paris without a blow, she came forward to protest against such dishonor. Her proposal to emancipate Paris from an infamous and treacherous government attracted the attention of the revolutionary leaders all through the days of the Commune.

Louise Michel shared their counsels and deliberations. The proudest moment of her life, no doubt, was the day when she put on the kepi and tunic of the National Guard, and with rifle on shoulder marched out against the troops from Versailles. Absolutely fearless, her presence alone would have sufficed to encourage the adherents of the most desperate cause. That she escaped death in this struggle for liberty was the more marvelous, as she did nothing to avoid it. She organized the central committee of women and fought in the ranks with even greater courage than did men, being severely wounded at the defense at Fort Isay. Before her wound healed, she was back at her post again. She was arrested and arraigned before the council at war. She made no defense and pleaded capital punishment. "I wished" she said,

> to oppose a barrier of flames to the invaders of Versailles, and if I failed it was no fault of my will or purpose. If it had been possible I should have killed theirs. I have no desire to live. I dedicated myself to France, and, unable to save her, death would be a boon. If you are not cowards, you will order my execution.

But besides her courage, Louise Michel had a great gift, a sense of humor wedded to a keen wit, which served her and her friends in the most desperate circumstances. Even in the terrible nights in the prison at Satory, when she heard and saw from the windows the fusillades tumbling batches of her comrades into the ditches that they had been forced to dig for themselves—even this did not quench her spirit.

With a bit of charcoal she cheered the drooping spirits of her fellow sufferers by drawing on the whitewashed walls absurd cari-caatures of the prison officials, until the latter begged the authorities to remove her as "incorrigible." Her resolute acceptance of all the responsibilities of the deeds with which she was accused at her trial is well known, but what her fellow exiles owed to her courage and cheerfulness on the long voyage to New Caledonia is not to be esti-mated. She herself returned to France firmly believing that all authority wielded by man over man was demoralizing; believing too, in the possibilities which lay before the human race through voluntary organization and the equal sharing of the goods and ills of life.

She never changed her attitude toward the wrongs and injustices met with everywhere; she did not become conservative or a compro-miser as so many do, when declining years are creeping upon them. Accused of inciting starving men to help themselves freely from the bake shops in the Boulevard St. Germain, she was again imprisoned in 1883 and again in 1886 for a revolutionary speech. At Havre, in 1888, she was shot at by an unemployed workingman while lectur-ing on the strikes, in which he was a sufferer. The bullet lodged in the back of her neck, but she covered the wound with her handkerchief and went on speaking, anxious only that her assailant should not be punished.

As she refused to give evidence against him, or allow her wound to be examined, the man was discharged, and when he died shortly afterwards of consumption, Louise Michel was one of his best friends. All those who escaped the awful butchery of the soldiers in the streets of Paris, during the last days of the Commune and who were known to have been at all active in that struggle were exiled to New Caledonia. The suffering of the prisoners in that pest hole was beyond description; at last a number of them were offered amnesty. Louise Michel was among the first who was offered pardon and transportation back to Paris; but she refused to leave while any remained, and stayed—nursing the sick and encouraging the weak in spirit.

She left the island only with the last batch who were released after years of torture. Such is the story in brief, and but poorly told, of the life of our noble comrade. The storm-tossed, ocean-beaten mariner struggles on and on amid the baffling waves, his courage is almost gone, but at last a light-house looms up in the far distance and he takes on fresh courage and strives on to reach it. So it is in the baffling ocean of humanity. A strong character like Louise Michel looms up like a pillar of light or a star of hope, and the weary reformer sees it and takes fresh courage to struggle on in the surging ocean of humanity, and endeavors to calm its troubled waves and point the way to the harbor of plenty.

Louise Michel died in Marseilles, France, January 9th, 1905, aged 73 years. We can but say, rest, sister and comrade, after your long and useful life; sweet sleep has come at last.

Chicago, The Liberator, October 29, 1905

PROPERTY RIGHTS *VS.* HUMAN RIGHTS

Every person who is rendering no good to humanity is useless, no matter how hard he works. Head work and hand work are equally hard and equally useful if rightly applied. All men, rich and poor, are working at something; perhaps one at useful labor, the other at useless labor. Nevertheless they are each and all using their energies at some occupation.

Men work because they cannot hold their physical and mental energies in check without causing themselves pain. But we have made work disagreeable because we have allowed conditions to obtain which force us to continue to work after we are tired, or at something for which we have no taste, take no interest in and have no adaptability for.

For this reason we lose pleasure in work and it becomes irksome to us; for this reason, often what we do is done in a slovenly manner and the community loses thereby. The selfish scheme called "property rights" has superseded human rights and created four times more useless work than is required to produce and distribute all the comforts and luxuries of life.

All these useless workers are either capitalists or the allies of capitalists. In this class of workers whose sole business is to sustain the "rights of property" can be classed the lawyers, jailers, police, bankers, insurance companies, agents and nearly all bosses in all branches of industry; add to these those who cannot get work and those in prisons, and we get some conception of the vast hordes that must be supported by those who perform useful labor, and these must devote their entire life's energies in keeping up the "rights of property," a thing which they have neither a share nor interest in. And this condition of affairs makes paupers, suicides, thieves, cutthroats, liars, vagabonds, hypocrites, and unsocial beings generally.

Who, pray, are benefitting by all this waste and confusion? The few, a mere small percentage of the population of the world. All the remainder submit, because they think "it always has been so and it must always be so." The work of those who have a conception of a true society of the future, must devote all their efforts toward disabusing the people's minds of the ancient falsehoods. It *can* be done. Many other hoary lies have passed away, so will this one, too.

Chicago, *The Liberator,* November 22, 1905

CRIME, VIOLENCE, AND SUICIDE

Under the heading of "Crime and Violence in 1905," a capitalist paper of this city gives some very interesting statistics:

> The record of homicides and of deaths occurring from various forms of violence during 1905 is not an encouraging one. . . . The approximate number of such deaths during the year now closing was 9,212, an increase of 730 over 1904. The most discouraging feature of the report is the continued increase of murders committed by burglars, thieves, and hold-up men. The number in 1905 was 582, as compared with 464 in 1904.

It will be seen that crimes committed in the attempt to get possession of other people's property (illegally) are on the increase.

Is this fact, sad as it is, without a cause?

Conditions make the man, not the man the conditions. Some day, when society has grown wise enough and just enough to make conditions pleasurable for her children, they will not be possessed of those low, brutal propensities which cause them to imbrue their hands in their brother's blood, but those who say these things are sneered at as "cranks and dreamers." So let it be; let the dreamer dream on—his dream will be realized some day, and then that generation will look back at us of today, their ancestors, as a lot of barbarians. It was ever thus: The dream of one century, if it contained truth and justice, became the actuality of the next century.

But the year 1905, with all its boasted prosperity (for the few), has a still sadder picture to present than the above. This is her suicide list:

> Suicide also continues to increase, the number of cases in 1905 being 9,982, as compared with 9,240 in 1904. The percentage of women who have committed suicide has increased. Last year there were nearly three times as many men as women, but this year there have been a little less than twice as many. It is appalling that suicide increases so rapidly. Despondency is the one great cause—despondency from sickness, life-failure, non-employment, bad luck, fatigue of living, and sometimes the conviction that life is not worth living.

Life, the "best boon to mortals given." To be, to feel the inspiring, vibrating currents of beautiful, bountiful Mother Nature playing all around us, through us; to feel oneself a part of a grand, magnificent whole, an entirety: Who could wish for more? Yet there are thousands (one every eighteen hours, our coroner informs us) out into the Great Unknown because they cannot longer endure the conditions of what ought to be a pleasant abiding place for man, but in his greed he has made it a veritable hell!

The Liberator, January 7, 1906

ANARCHY:
The Negative of Government

W̶e are told that the word Anarchy needs constant explanation; that whenever used in its literal sense it must be defined. Is there any other word of which this is not true? The introduction of new ideas into a man's mind is not accompanied by the use of a specially coined word, but by the adaptation of old words to broader uses. Even the word self-government would not convey our meaning in its broadest generalization. This word has been understood since its introduction into general use to mean a system of representative government—the delegation of personal rights to be represented by another person deemed to be the highest approach of liberty possible in a state.

In seeking the establishment, not of a system of government, but of the greater extension of liberty, the use of this word would be far more objectionable than the word Anarchy, and this because it carries with it a recognition of government and the necessity of political action; Earl Derby boasted when Premier in the House of Lords of England's "principles of popular government."

In every instance in which Americans use the word "self-government" it carries with it the idea of representation as well as administration. States in the Union by their "residuary rights" possess self-government, and individuals enjoy the fullest self-government; the trouble is, liberty has not yet acquired a substantive tutelage of past ages, has not been outgrown so largely, but

LUCY E. PARSONS
(Widow of ALBERT R. PARSONS one of the
HAYMARKET MEETING MARTYRS of CHICAGO.)

WILL DELIVER FOUR LECTURES AT
Jefferson Square Hall
925 Golden Gate Avenue

June 15th, 8 p. m.—"The Labor Movement in America for the Past Fifty Years."

June 22d, 8 p. m.—"Woman's Progress."

June 29th, 8 p. m.—"The French Revolution, What it Accomplished."

July 6th, 8 p. m.—"The True Story of the Haymarket Riot and the Great Eight Hour Strike of 1886."

ADMISSION 15c

Mrs. Parsons has been an active worker in the Labor Movement for over 30 years. :: :: :: ::

Publicity for a Lecture Series
(San Francisco, 1910s)

that the halo of authority still lingers around all our words.

Nevertheless, humanity tends always more and more toward individualism, that is toward *real* self-government, which is the only true, just and sane government. Today we are passing out of political into economic problems, over which the state has no influence, being the *creature* of existing economic conditions; hence, a word is needed which, while not condemning administration, will unequivocally express opposition to political government. The old bottles answered to hold the old wine of politics. Economic questions, not being solvable by political methods, demand new bottles for the new ideas time evolves.

Government is stationary, social growth is progressive; consequently we find ourselves arrived at a point where governments become a barrier to economic progress. True, this position is a reversal of the common accepted belief, which is that government is a help to progress. But a close study of the origin, tendency and operations of all governments will show that they *never* lead to progress.

Governments always stand for the "established order of things." Hence, we use the word *anarchy*, the negative of government, and will retain it when the political state has merged into the social commonwealth.

The Liberator, February 3, 1906
original title, "Anarchism"

AGITATION TRIP

To Comrades and Friends: It is my intention to go East on an agitation trip in a week or two. I will deliver lectures upon the following subjects: "Curse of Child Labor," "The Commune," "Anarchism Defined," "The Industrial Workers of the World: Their Aims and Object." Comrades will please arrange meetings and communicate with me as soon as possible.

The Liberator, March 11, 1906; original title, "Trip East"

WHO WERE THE MOLLY MAGUIRES?

W ho were the Molly Maguires? So much is said and written about them at the present time, and so little seems to be known of their origin, aims and objects, even by the labor press, who, aping the capitalist press, speak of them as "bandits," thus implying that they were marauders or terrorists of some kind, composed only of murderers who the Pinkerton thug, McParland, broke up, getting a number of them hung, thus doing a great service to society at large.

Now, *really*, who were the Molly Maguires?

Let us cross the ocean to the soil of Ireland to ascertain who they were. In the fifties and sixties, and into the seventies of the last century, everyone at all familiar with history is aware of the terrible conditions prevailing among the masses in that landlord-cursed country. They know how gaunt famine stared the people in the face, yet the landlords exacted their very hearts' blood. When the tenants couldn't pay rent for the abominable little shacks which they occupied, owing to their poverty, caused by the failure of crops, they were flung bodily out, together with their belongings upon the highways and, to prevent their entering the shanty, it was razed to the ground.

A gang of fellows went along with the constabulary, carrying crowbars for the purposes of destroying the huts, just as soon as the families had been thrown out. These men were called the "crowbar brigade." On a certain day in 1866, a number of constables and the "crowbar brigade" started out on a mission of eviction. In the course of their rounds, they arrived at the shanty of a poor tenant by the name of Pat Maguire, and proceeded to throw his family out. Mrs Maguire was in child-bed confinement, but this made no difference to the hard-hearted villains, they proceeded to throw her and the newborn baby out. This conduct enraged the neighbors so that they rallied to the aid of Maguire, beat the constables and the "crowbar brigade" off, and reinstated the man's sick wife and baby in the "home."

From that time hence, all who opposed the encroachments of the landlord's hirelings were called "Molly Maguires." Between the years, 1848 to about 1870, thousands of Ireland's sons and daugh-

116

ters emigrated so that there were more Irish in this country than there were in Ireland. Thousands of these immigrants found their way into the coalfields of Pennsylvania. Up to this time, the coal mines had been operated by Americans whose standard of life was higher than that of a lot of famine stricken people.

The Americans, for a time, made a feeble resistance to the encroachment, but the mine owners wanted cheap labor, regardless of nationality; the Americans had to go. In the course of a few years, a still cheaper class of labor began to find its way into the coal fields, *viz.*, the Slavs, Hungarians and others from Southern Europe. The Irish quite naturally objected to being thus displaced.

They formed some kind of a Molly Maguire organization in the anthracite regions, for the purpose of keeping out those who were under-bidding them in the labor market, and in a measure, they were succeeding; this enraged the capitalists, but they did not seem able to get into the councils of the "Molly Maguires," so they employed McParland (who is just now posing as a great factor in running to earth "conspiracies" in Colorado and Idaho).

This McParland went into the coal mines as a miner. For two years he worked with the miners as one of them; the illustrated book, issued by the Pinkertons some years ago, showed him as chief mourner at the funerals, best man at the weddings, a swell fellow well met with the men; drinking whiskey from the same bottle, and all the time weaving strands of hope that were to hang them! At last a number of the most active men were arrested. McParland produced his "evidence", a capitalist jury did the rest.

Thirty-eight miners were executed, thirteen in one day. The men, having no organization to defend them, were soon frightened into slavery, where they remained for a quarter of a century or more, on until the rise and strength of the United Mine Workers of America.

Such in brief is a history of the "Molly Maguires," which was an organization (if organization it could be called), attempting in a poor, weak, stumbling way, to combat the greed of capital. And such, also, is a brief story of the past villainy of the villain McParland, who now turns up to swear away the lives of other innocent men: Moyer, Haywood and their comrades.

With such a hardened, conscienceless wretch as this McParland

117

will have a hard fight for their lives; they will need lots of money —many thousands of dollars. *The Liberator* begs all lovers of justice and fair play, regardless of party or creed, to send as much money as they can possibly share, to John M. O'Neill,* Pioneer Building, Denver, Colorado.

The Liberator, March 11, 1906

CAPITALIST CONSPIRACY IN IDAHO

The American people, and especially the working class, do not seem to realize the importance of and the class interest involved in the arrest of Moyer, Haywood and Pettibone. If these, our brothers in labor's cause, are to be saved from the gallows, there must be a tremendous amount of agitation carried on. Money must be raised, and lots of it, for their defense. The working class must be made aware of the long fight between the Mine Owners' Association and the Western Federation of Miners, and shown the connection between this struggle and these arrests.

Anarchists cannot afford to be backward in this matter. Many of us have passed through the awful ordeal and know what anguish it is to those men and their families. If there is not to be another slaughter like that of twenty years ago in Chicago, systematic agitation must go steadily forward from now on.

While on my trip in the East, I propose to do my share in arousing the people to a realization of the infamy of the conspiracy. I shall address mass-meetings upon this subject.

The Liberator, March 25, 1906

CRIME AND CRIMINALS

Our saintly Christians and other goody-goody people throw up their hands in horror, in contemplating the prevalence of crime among the "lower classes." Crimes, or unsociable acts among the "lower classes," are only a reflex of crimes or robberies of the upper or "better classes." We rob our children before they are born. How many thousands, yea millions, of mothers among the working class are there who see a thousand and one articles while in a state of pregnancy which their appetite craves or their heart desires, and yet are unable to gratify it? They walk the streets, gazing at the gorgeous displays, everything to attract the eye and cause the heart to wish for, yet unable, owing to poverty, to gratify such natural longings. What is the consequence?

The unborn child is impressed, it feels the same disappointment that the mother feels; it is impressed upon it. We have robbed it before its birth, it enters the world with an unsatisfied, grasping nature. This proclivity grows steadily upon it with its growing years; the desire grows stronger because of poverty, and, finally, the child reaches forth and takes some one else's property. This is theft, it is illegally done; then society for the first time takes an interest in this human being. It comes forward to punish the child, it is now ready to inflict torture upon the victim of its own false, unnatural, inhuman system. How much better, wiser and cheaper it would have been to make conditions natural and social so that the child could have seen the light of Earth under the best conditions possible, instead of—as is often the case—under the worst conditions.

How much better this would be than to have to build great, gloomy prisons, superintended by guardsmen, who harden and debase their natures still more. And the case holds good with murders, legal and illegal, or lynchings. The sensational press gives all the gory details of such occurrences in great glaring headlines. They catch the eye of thousands of prospective mothers; they are impressed by the horror and its details, and they in turn impress the unborn child. The child is born, it reaches man's and woman's estate, some adversity crosses its path, and the old prenatal impression rushes upon it and an awful deed is committed! The community is shocked and wonders where such a monster could have come from. Another candidate starts for the prison or the gallows. Thus the long procession is ever wending its way through the ages. The hoary-headed old hag, society, throws up her hands in "holy" horror when one of her children commits an awful deed. She never recognizes the fact that this is only the reflex of her own misdeeds. Crime is simply a social disease.

When society has grown wise enough to supplant the prison with the schoolhouse, the teacher for the hangman and kind treatment for punishment and substituting justice and kindness for brutality, we will hear very little more about "crime and criminals."

The Liberator, March 25, 1906

THE IWW AND THE SHORTER WORKDAY

The utter irreconcilability of the interest of labor and capital based upon the present system of buying and selling: the utter hopelessness of arbitrating and harmonizing the interests of the two parties to any lasting agreement, one of whom gains where the other loses, should be transparent to any one who gives the matter serious thought. We see this fact exemplified now in the long wrangle going on between the miners and the mine owners. Capital is invested in a "plant" by its owner for the purpose of deriving profit therefrom.

Labor is employed to reproduce or create more wealth, and the mutual interests of wealth-producer and the profit-taker is ended. The one is employed by the other; the laborer wishes to sell his labor at the highest figure possible; the capitalist wishes to buy at the lowest, so the conflict of interest begins. The whole labor problem is brought up when the dispute arises over the share of the product which each of these parties, the workers and the capitalists, are to receive. The competitive system fixes the wages received by the wage class upon the basis of mere subsistence; all over and above this sum, the surplus, goes to the profit-taker. Hence the hours of labor is a vital question at all times, for it is a well established fact that the compensation of the wage-earner decreases in exact proportion to the number of hours he is employed, while the share of the profit-taker increases in the same ratio.

This is not taking into account the moral and social benefits to be derived from the added leisure gained by shorter work days. The capitalistic class understands this; consequently there is no demand for a reduction of the working hours. Witness the long, hard fight for this point alone. A reduction of the hours of labor to the point where all can have employment is worth a General Strike, because upon this point all efforts can be focused, and if carried, its beneficial effects would be felt immediately by the whole working class, men, women and children.

It would be an object lesson at once demonstrating what united effort can accomplish. Having carried this point of attack, further moves could be instituted for attacks upon the profit-taking class, and gained until the wage system is abolished and a system of co-operation is instituted, the working class preparing themselves in the meantime for a larger liberty.

There was a movement at one time, not so many years ago either, which was international in its scope, which had for its object the setting aside the first of May for a general, international holiday, looking ultimately to the inauguration of a short-hour workday, but this grand idea has been side-tracked in later years by a lot of political buncombe and claptrap, thus persuading the working classes into the notion that they can gain their freedom by electing a lot of fellows to office.

The IWW and other advanced labor organizations could not show their real usefulness to the toiling classes better than by reviving this international holiday. For the IWW cannot hope to gain and hold the confidence of the wage class long if it has no definite aim in view looking to a lasting betterment of economic conditions. The Industrial Workers of the World have been organized nearly a year. What have they done worth mentioning? Carried a few isolated, insignificant strikes? What does this amount to? The whole organization seems to be floundering around like a ship lost at sea without a rudder. Take the magazine, *The Industrial Worker*. Three issues are out. There is no definite line of action outlined in it. What kind of showing can they make at their next convention soon to be held?*

The Liberator, April 8, 1906

NEW YORK LETTER

After a long run from Chicago, one arrives in Jersey City. You take a ferry boat for New York City. The Hudson River is fairly swarming with crafts of every description, from the small tug to the great trans-Atlantic steamer, the wonder of maritime achievements. After a few minutes we touch the New York shore; then we are ushered into the most intense center of commercialism on this continent—the most intense poverty and the most luxuriating wealth.

Here we have our Murray Hill, Fifth Avenue, Riverside Drive and Madison Avenue, etc., with their magnificent palaces, equipages, fine women and fancy dogs, the latter much in evidence. The people who dwell along these avenues lack nothing so much as human kindness and a realization that they are a part and parcel of a common humanity; they have their troubles, cares and sorrows, it is true, but these are due largely to the unnatural lives they lead; it is a different care and sorrow from that of the poor.

Speaking of the poor, I have seen more abject poverty within a stone's throw of where I am stopping, and in walking through the streets where live the poor of New York City, than I have witnessed in the whole course of my life before.

In coming to New York, I passed through miles and miles of as good rich, tillable land as there is to be found anywhere, both in the United States and Canada. Millions of acres of this land are untouched, and when I arrive in New York I find tens of thousands of human beings living in heaps, piled upon one another, packed like sardines in tenement houses, poor, ignorant and dejected, helpless-

122

ness and despair deep-furrowed upon their blank faces. Every steamship which lands, dumps hundreds of them each day upon the streets of New York City, and these float towards and become mixed in with the poverty already here, until the whole mass presents a picture of poverty and despair at once degrading, disgusting and depressing. It cannot be duplicated anywhere in America, I believe.

In short, the evils and glaring inequalities of conditions under our present unjust, unsocial system are more conspicuous here than anywhere else in America, is my candid belief. Here tens of thousands of children are born each year, doomed to be reared in the stuffy, dirty, overcrowded tenements and upon the dirty streets and sidewalks, who will never know what the beauties of nature mean, will never know what it is to lie beneath a shady tree and watch the fleeing clouds flit by or hear the songbird sing, or watch the green leaves with which the gentle breezes play, or sit beside the babbling brook and build air-castles.

No! All the charms of nature in her purity will remain to them a sealed book. Alas! None of these innocent pastimes will ever be enjoyed by thousands of New York City's children. From the bare, barren, uninviting tenements they will go to the factories and become mere cogs in the great revolving wheels. Their intellects, already stupefied, will become brutalized. How to get these help-less human beings out of the overcrowded cities and on the bosom of Mother Earth is one of the greatest problems of the age. In the streets and quarters where dwell the poor, there is no evidence of race suicide. In the house where I am stopping, there are six fami-lies to the floor; the building is six stories high; there is but one entrance to the whole house. The only places for the children to play are in the halls and street, or on the stairs.

This is one of the modern houses; in fact, it is just completed. The bedrooms are so small that only single beds or cots can be used in them. Into these little flats will often be crowded four, five or six families, dear reader. I only give the facts. If President Roosevelt were to happen into this part of the town, his dentistry would shine forth resplendently; he would see no signs of race suicide hereabout. Living expenses are something unthinkable to those who have never visited New York. For four small rooms—

mere closets—on the fourth or fifth floors, $25 is paid; for the lower floors, still more is paid, higher rents are charged. All the necessaries of life are at exorbitant prices.

When these prices are taken into account one can imagine how the people are compelled to crowd together in order to pay the rent and live at all. But, readers of *The Liberator*, here is the best joke of the season on your humble correspondent:

Two days after arriving in New York City I started out to do a little "slumming" and to gather material for *The Liberator*. Well, I strolled leisurely along Broom Street (which needs brooms very badly), noting the evidences of wretchedness that are to be seen on every hand.

Duplications of the countenance of the "The Man with a Hoe" are met on all sides in these quarters of the town, these streets of the Ghetto. At a newsstand I stopped, purchased a morning paper, was about to fasten my handbag when I was suddenly, rudely jostled, and my handbag was "swiped" by a light-fingered gentle-man—an "artful dodger" who made off with my handbag: money, valuables and all. So sudden was the hold, in broad daylight, that I was amazed. I tried to follow the robber, but my way was blocked by two others.

Then I understood the whole scheme. I was the victim of a gang who had been following me, waiting for a favorable opportunity to snatch my handbag. Well, for a few minutes I was bewildered. A thousand miles from home, not a penny, and hungry at that, for I was on my way to lunch at the time. The thief was twenty dollars ahead; I was twenty dollars out of pocket. I felt very humble indeed. The Ghetto lost all interest for me.

Reader, were you ever in the same fix? I hope you never may be. When I related my troubles to my friends, the New Yorkers—they had a very cold, discomforting way about them. They said, in a distant, nonchalant way, "Why, didn't you know you were in New York?"

New York, nevertheless, is a great and wonderful city. It is liable to take considerable of the conceit out of a Chicagoan to come here.

The Liberator, April 8, 1906

NEW YORK STREET VENDORS
A Day in the Ghetto: Once Seen, Never Forgotten

You may read of an ocean voyage, you may peruse the best books on travel, you may lay the book down and congratulate yourself that you know as much about an ocean trip as though you had crossed it in person. This was what I once thought, but one must have experienced the sensation of being on a great oceanliner, you must feel the roll of the mighty billows beneath you, you must count the stars at night in mid-ocean, with only the firmament above and the vast expanse of water below, and hear the throb of the hearts of the mighty engines, and dream of the continent which you are leaving and the one that you are nearing, or see the sun rise and cast its rays upon the broad expanse of an ocean waste. You must feel that calmness of spirit and relaxation of nervous tension which only an ocean voyage brings. To be able to realize a storm at sea, you must lie in your berth and hear the great waves dash madly above you, feel the ship's "dip" and wonder if she will ever "right" herself again. One must be ocean-tossed, storm-beaten, to know what it is; at least this was my experience.

Turning from the ocean of water to the ocean of humanity it is the same thing. One must see it to realize what it is.

Many of you have doubtless read of the poverty of New York City's "submerged" population; of its Ghetto population; of what the settlement workers are doing to relieve the poor of the East Side. But in order to get a true conception of what it is, you must come to New York City, and stroll along Hester, Chrystie, lower Bowery, Broom and a few other streets. You must witness these waves of poverty as they roll from the packed tenements up from the basements, casements, upon the narrow, filthy sidewalks, along which stand long lines of garbage cans over-running with their ill-assorted contents, which in hot weather emit odors at once disgusting and unhealthy. The narrow streets and sidewalks fairly swarm with dirty children and frowsy-haired women.

The more poverty-stricken the appearance of the women, the greater the number of children they seem to have clinging to their skirts. Along against the sidewalks of the Ghetto are pushcarts

125

from which vendors offer for sale practically every article under the sun—dishes, glassware, bric-a-brac, hardware, dry-goods of every description, groceries, fruits, vegetables, meats; in short, everything from matches—two boxes for a cent—to a set of furniture. Talk about your streets of Cairo in Egypt, or Jerusalem, etc., to be seen in World's Fairs: They are as nothing compared to the streets of the Ghetto of New York City. There are more people living in a given space in New York City than any other spot on Earth, not excepting Peking, China. Mercy, though!

One doesn't realize the vast numbers of people living in this city until between five and six p.m. Then the tall factories belch forth their quota of human beings; then along the streets the long procession begins to wind its weary way; men, women and children (but not many of the latter) crowd the sidewalks until fully one-third must take to the streets because room on the sidewalk is out of the question. This excessively crowded condition doesn't last long, however. Very soon the great tenements have swallowed what the factories emitted. Hurrying home, these people partake of their meager meal in stuffy little rooms, retire early in order to rest for the next day's round of toil. This is the routine of life of hundreds of thousands of New York City's population. This is the downtown condition.

Uptown, where dwell the rich robbers, masters of slaves, how different is all this! Presto change-o! All is wealth, luxury, quietude, and ease.

Meanwhile, the spirit of revolution is making progress, slow but sure. Some day retributive justice will take a hand; it will reach upward and tear down that which is base, vile, despotic, plutocratic and domineering. Reaching downward, she will lift the fallen, despoiled, robbed and weak. We will not then have rich idlers or poverty-stricken workers, but a fully rounded out humanity. Our "slum" districts are a curse to our civilization. They must go!

What beautiful lives these teeming millions might live if only that spirit, "Do unto others as you would have others do unto you," would prevail.

The Liberator, April 15, 1906

THE IMPORTANCE OF A PRESS

There is no way of building up a movement, strengthening it and keeping it intact, except by a press, at least weeklies, if dailies are impossible. The press is the medium through which we exchange ideas, keep abreast of the times, take the gauge of battle and see how far the class conflict has progressed. It is by the press we educate the public mind and link the people of most distant parts together in bonds of fraternity and comradeship. We can keep track of the work and accomplishments of our comrades in no other way, except by the medium of paper. *The Liberator* is the only English-language anarchist propaganda paper in America; for this reason, comrades and sympathizers in all parts of the country should feel in duty bound to support this paper, write for it, contribute to its support financially, and make its success their personal concern.

The expense of carrying on a paper that costs as little as *The Liberator* does is trifling, if only a few active spirits would interest themselves in its welfare. There was never a time in the history of America when there was such urgent need for radical education as at the present moment. The rich are becoming more oppressive, domineering and arrogant each day; the people more depressed, despoiled and helpless. Every radical should try to reach them and educate them to a correct understanding of their condition in society; tell them why they are exploited, and the remedy. *The Liberator* is trying to perform this task.

Comrades, will you help us?

The Liberator, April 19, 1906

THE HAYWOOD TRIAL
and the Anarchist Trial

There has been no event in recent years which has shown the advance made in class-conscious labor organizations more distinctly than the class trial just ended in Boise, Idaho, and its comparison with the trial of the Anarchists at Chicago in 1886.

The Anarchist trial was a class trial—relentless, vindictive, savage and bloody. By that prosecution the capitalists sought to break the great strike for the eight-hour day which was being successfully inaugurated in Chicago, this city being the storm-center of that great movement; and they also intended, by the savage manner in which they conducted the trial of these men, to frighten the working class back to their long hours of toil and low wages from which they were attempting to emerge. The capitalistic class imagined they could carry out their hellish plot by putting to an ignominious death the most progressive leaders among the working class of that day. In executing their bloody deed of judicial murder they succeeded, but in arresting the mighty onward movement of the class struggle they utterly failed.

So, too, in the trial just ended at Boise, Idaho, they wished to break up that magnificent organization, the Western Federation of Miners, by foully murdering, under the forms of law, its valiant officers and champions—Moyer, Haywood and Pettibone.

The stage-setting, preparatory for the enactment of this capitalistic conspiracy, was about the same as it was in the case of the Chicago Anarchists. There was the Pinkerton liar with his pockets bulging out with "evidence." In the Anarchists' case it was the eight-hour movement to be suppressed; in the Haywood case it was the Western Federation of Miners they were after, and they wanted to make an example of its leaders.

But, lo and behold, the class-conscious wage class, which has come into existence since 1886, had not been reckoned with by the conspirators, and the radical press, which was to keep them posted, had also been overlooked. The capitalistic class began to juggle around in the law courts. This proved their undoing, because it gave the working class time to get together and take council, and then the workers realized in what great peril their brothers stood, and began to understand what a great consolidation of capitalistic interests they must make a stand against. They also realized it was money, and plenty of it, that must be collected, and the best legal talent secured, and that they should have a press which would truthfully report the proceedings of the case.

All these were denied our comrades in 1886-87. The only papers friendly to them were seized and suppressed by the authorities. The labor organizations were young, undisciplined, and had no money in their treasuries. The capitalistic press and pulpit thundered their foul slander against these victims until they succeeded in blinding the eyes and closing the ears of the public to reason, and they completed the conspiracy by packing the jury and obtaining one of the most prejudiced judges who ever presided at a trial.

Under these circumstances is it any wonder that our comrades were railroaded to the scaffold? Why, it only took that precious jury three hours to bring in a verdict of "guilty," sending eight innocent men to the gallows. The presiding judge had the brazen effrontery to tell the jury from the bench that they deserved to be compensated for the verdict!

How changed is the public conscience in these times of the year of 1907, all owing to the growing intelligence of the working class and their alertness in coming to the rescue of their brothers. To verify this fact, let anyone who cares to take the trouble contrast the charge of Judge Gary, in the Anarchists' case, with that of Judge Wood in the Haywood trial. Gary's was prejudiced and vindictive to the last degree, while Judge Wood's was calm, cool and fair. The attorneys in the case of the Anarchists requested Gary to instruct the jury in regard to the degrees of murder—murder in the second degree, manslaughter, etc.—but the bloodthirsty old villain would have nothing but murder in the first degree.

The last twenty years of my life—since that dark, sad November 11, 1887, when my dear husband and his comrades fell victims to a capitalistic conspiracy—have suddenly become a great pleasure to me, because I see in the Haywood verdict the tendency of the advanced thought of these times, and I realize that their lives were not sacrificed in vain. They only lived twenty years too soon.

For the first time in American history the working class was united and stood shoulder to shoulder. They became "class conscious" in recognizing the fact that it was not Haywood the mine-owners were really after, but the labor organization that he represented.

While we are holding our jubilees over the complete routing of the whole "bunch," let us not forget that we still have to deal with a crafty, cunning, unprincipled set of rascals who, smarting from their defeat, are still thirsting for innocent blood. Let us remember that Moyer and Pettibone are still in their clutches and the Pinkerton plague is still at large in society, and possibly there is another Orchard* in the perspective. While we rejoice over the Haywood verdict, let us be ever watchful lest these, our brothers, fall victims of class war.

The Demonstrator (Lakebay, WA), September 4, 1907

A WISE MOVE:
On Anarchist Organization

The recent Congress of Anarchists, held at Amsterdam, Holland, seems to me to be a wise move and a step in the right direction.

The Anarchistic cause (there has been no *movement* in recent years) has lacked a plan of procedure or organization. To be sure, there have somehow, here and there, drifted together a few persons who, in a loose way, formed a sort of group, calling themselves Anarchists, but these groups were composed, for the most part, of young, inexperienced people who had about as many conceptions of the real aims of Anarchism as there were members composing the group; consequently, the result has been as might reasonably have been expected. The anarchistic cause has lacked concentration of effort, and a vivifying force to lend energy and direction toward a common aim.

The result is that the realization of the anarchistic ideal, grand as it is, is not in the least encouraging when we take a retrospective view of the last twenty years. Really, what evidence have we of a genuine growth of Anarchism in the last twenty years? There has not been in that time a single work produced by an original writer. A few pamphlets only have been written. All the weekly and monthly publications have had short leases of life, with struggling, starving existences—that is, in the English language. London *Freedom* is the single exception.

I, personally, have always held to the idea of organization, together with an assumption of responsibility by the members, such as paying monthly dues and collecting funds for propaganda purposes. For holding these views, I have been called an "old-school" Anarchist, etc.

Turning from the past to the future, I most sincerely hope that the recent congress is the beginning of a new era for Anarchism. I trust that this country and the world will resound with the grand truths of Anarchism—the right of every man and woman upon this Earth, who contributes to the marvelous and diversified products, to their share in the same; and that to be really free is to allow each one to live their lives in their own way so long as each allows all to do the same.

Anarchism teaches that no one is made better by the enactment of laws, but many crimes and unsocial acts are purely the result of official meddling to make people "good" by law.

Anarchism, as taught in recent years, is too far away from the mental level of the masses; hence, they have not been attracted to us. Our enemies have put their own interpretation upon our ideas, and we are in no condition to defend ourselves because we have no press. I trust this condition will soon change and we will have a movement in fact instead of one only in name.

Yours for the social revolution,
    Lucy E. Parsons

Letter to the Editor, *The Demonstrator,* November 6, 1907

INDUSTRIAL WORKERS OF THE WORLD:
Aims and Objects

The Industrial Workers of the World, an organization launched in Chicago last June, is making wonderful progress in all parts of the country, and in practically every industry. This is as it should be, because the IWW is organized along the lines of the evolution of capitalism, which is so organized, that under one head or one management, whole lines of industry are conducted, reaching from ocean to ocean or from Maine to Mexico. So that the freight-handler working in the freight yards in San Francisco is affected when the longshoreman in New York City asks for better conditions from the employer, and he must be prepared to back his brother up in his just demand.

It is the mission of the IWW to teach the laboring classes their solidarity of interest as a mass and, how they in future must act as a class, in order to win in their contests with capital. The line of action of the IWW is in direct contrast to that of the AF L, whose members are compelled to "scab" on each other when a strike of any dimension is declared, as was the case during the late teamsters' strike in Chicago, where the freight-handlers had to receive, handle and ship goods delivered to them by scab teamsters.

Had these laborers belonged to the IWW, the freight-handlers, shipping clerks, teamsters and all others belonging to the shipping department would have refused absolutely to handle the scab-delivered goods. This drastic action would have brought on a crisis at once. The battle would have been short, sharp and decisive, and the teamsters would not have been compelled to pass through the long struggle of broken heads, fines, injunctions, etc., and at last forced to surrender, because the cry of their hungry children was too much for their manly hearts to stand. It will be the same old game of union member scabbing on union member next spring, if the miners strike.

Then will be witnessed the spectacle of the other members of the AFL handling scab-mined coal. This must continue to be the case as long as labor is organized as crafts instead of as a class. *The Liberator* advises all working men and women to investigate the principles and plan of organization of the Industrial Workers of the World.

The Liberator, November 22, 1907

A STROLL THROUGH THE STREETS
OF CHICAGO

Since the sudden stoppage of the big wheel in Wall Street, which is the center of the capitalistic universe, havoc has been played in the industrial ranks generally. The wheels in the factories have ceased to revolve, the fires have been drawn, and hundreds of thousands of the wage-earning class have been, and are being, thrown upon the highways in the country and the city streets.

Reader, can you realize its effects? Maybe not, so let us take a stroll through the streets of this wonderful city of Chicago.

It is two p.m. The afternoon papers are just out; a thousand or more people are buying them, perhaps paying out their last penny. They read the "ads" eagerly; off they dash pell mell in a mad race, trying to outstrip each other in their mad rush to reach the job. So many appear at the place that the boss has to close the door to prevent its being carried away by storm.

This is no overdrawn picture; it actually occurs every day in hundreds of places in this city, and of course in hundreds of other cities.

The free coffee wagons and soup kitchens are in full operation, and all the police stations and cheap lodging-houses are filled to suffocation. Charity is the dope being handed out by the robber class at present to the poor people to keep them quiet, and it is successful at least for the time being.

Coffee wagons, soup kitchens and cheap lodging-houses are being patronized by men only. What has become of the women? About as many women as men were discharged. To the "underworld" they soon will sink, some of them never to rise again!

And this panic is only two months old! What, in the name of justice, is in store for us in the near future?

In the face of these hellish conditions there are radicals who preach to us about peace, intellectual education, and the like. Why should all the lamblike peace be on the side of the working class? Why should they be quiet while starving or receiving just sufficient for their laborious toil to keep body and soul together and to produce more slaves for the bosses? The spirit of resistance seems to have forsaken the working class.

I believe in peace at any price—except at the price of liberty. But this precious gift the wealth-producers already seem to have lost. Life—mere existence—they have; but what is life worth when it lacks those elements which make for enjoyment?

Advocating peace is a good thing in its way; but, like many other things, it can be overworked.

In this city there are fully 100,000 persons out of employment, and the number is on the increase.

The Demonstrator, January 16, 1908 (excerpts); original title: "The Wheel of Fortune"

REFLECTIONS OF A PROPAGANDIST

I have been here in New York City for the last three months, selling the famous speeches of the Chicago martyrs. Here humanity is piled up in heaps, stored away in layers; forty families in a single tenement that should only suffice for a fourth that number.

In these Eastern cities, tens of thousands of children are born annually who will never know the beauties of nature. From the tenement they will have for playing space the hard, dirty, unhealthy, stone sidewalks and pavements, then a few years in school, where the training will be as inadequate to the development of a strong, self-asserting individuality as were the previous conditions to the upbuilding of a strong, physical body; then comes the last step, the factory, the slave pen. From there some will graduate to prisons, some to the hangman, and some become prostitutes, offering upon the streets, for a price, the remnant of a depleted body. This is the goal toward which the long procession of the working class is ever moving. Is the picture overdrawn? None could wish more sincerely than the writer that it is imaginary, but alas, it is too terribly true.

I have before me two reports from committees, returned in the last few days from New York City. One states there were "born in the city in 1910 8,750 children of weak minds, and that this tendency is ever on the increase." The other, that something will have to be done to check the alarming overcrowding of tenements. There is no overcrowding uptown, where the rich live.

I met with very courteous treatment from the unions in the West and am meeting with the same here. I have credentials and endorsement from the Central Federated Union, and my success is splendid in the locals. But I find organized labor weak and dispirited. I have called the attention of several leaders to this fact, and asked for an explanation. They simply say: "You have no Ellis Island problem in the West to solve as we have here."

I think there is a lot of reason in this position. For the countless thousands form a never-ending stream of humanity, dumped down in a strange land, hearing a strange language, with little money or means of a livelihood, they fall an easy prey to the sharks, little and big, and are used as an instrument to beat down and keep wages near the dead line of want.

The revolutionary societies of New York City held a very successful memorial meeting in honor of our Japanese martyrs.* The large hall was packed and the speeches were good and to the point. After the speaking had been going on for a few hours, some of the young blood in the hall wanted to see the speeches translated into action. One of them went to the front and called upon the audience to go to the street, fall in line, and march upon the Japanese Embassy and voice their protest.

There was some opposition to the carrying out of this part of the meeting, but the young blood carried everything before it. The result was a fine demonstration in the streets, with the red flag. The only time the red flag ever typifies death is at the time of the death of a martyr to liberty; then it is appropriately draped in mourning, as it was on this occasion. Of course the capitalist press made heroes of the police and also got themselves all worked up to a great sensation.

The only regret I have about the street demonstration is owing to a misunderstanding and the slow exit of the large audience, I missed being with the "mob" of marchers. I have been kicking myself about this ever since.

The Agitator, March 1, 1911

THE MOVING INSPIRATION OF OUR AGE

Our comrades [the Haymarket Martyrs] sleep the sleep which knows no awakening, but the grand cause for which they died is not asleep nor dead: It is the live, inspiring issue of every land and clime where the ray of civilization has penetrated. It is the moving inspiration of our age, the only question worth struggling for: the question of how to lift humanity from poverty and despair.

This question is the swelling tide of our age. It is useless for the ruling class to stand on the shore of discontent and attempt to force this tide back to its depths of poverty, for it swells up from the hearts of the people. And though they should erect gallows along all the highways and byways, build prisons and increase armies, the tide will continue to rise until it overwhelms them in a worldwide revolution. This is the lesson of history.

From "The Trial a Farce," The Agitator, November 15, 1911

THE EIGHT-HOUR STRIKE OF 1886

The Industrial Workers of the World is the last child born of the great surging struggle in the world's arena between labor and capital. It is a child vigorous and aggressive, gaining in strength, expanding in power, and commanding attention and respect. This young child is the progeny of a long line of the Earth's stalwarts who have engaged in the onward march towards a better world.

The IWW is urging the workers to set aside the first of May, 1912 to demand of the master class an eight-hour working day. Of course if the working class are not sufficiently awake to their own interests to come out and stand like men for this very just and modest demand, the IWW will not abandon the agitation; on the contrary, it may agitate for a still shorter work day, so as to keep pace, to some extent at least, with the advance in labor-saving (labor-destroying) machinery. A reduction of the working time is the most just and practical palliative that can be injected into the issue between labor and capital. In fact, while it seems to be a palliative on the face of it, it is in reality not a palliative at all, but a revolutionary measure, because time is the greatest factor in our existence.

It has taken eons of time to develop every particle of matter in the universe, man included, yet time to man is so short and precious. There is so little that he can accomplish between the time that his mother implants her first mother-love kiss upon his newborn cheek to when death has clasped him in its cold embrace. If he has run his two- or three-score years between the cradle and the grave, and has occupied every moment of that time to the very best advantage possible, he has accomplished very little indeed.

It would be well if the working class would heed the call of the IWW and cease to labor on the first day of May and take stock of themselves and try to realize what space of time elapses from the time they offer their labor to the boss, at about fifteen years—in other words, when they place their capital on the market, "capital" which consists of stored-up power in their muscles and brains—to their forty-fifth or fiftieth year, when the best there was in them has been used up by the boss and they are flung out upon the human scrap-heap as useless material, with nothing more to be ground out of them for the benefit of the boss.

I say it will be well for them to stop for one day at least, and take stock of their stock—that is of themselves, and see if it is worth while for them to spend three-fourths of their time toiling for a bare existence: not for a *living*, for the vast majority of them do not live, they barely exist. If they should stop to think they would soon better their condition.

The first great strike of America for a reduction of hours of labor to eight per day occurred on May First, 1886. In October 1885, a convention of labor organizations was held in Chicago; at said convention a resolution was passed, requesting the working class to set aside the First of May, 1886, to demand a reduction of the hours of the workers to eight. The Knights of Labor was not represented at the above mentioned convention and did not parti-

137

cipate in the strike as a national organization, but many of the [Knights'] "Assemblies" did so. The radical element in Chicago were divided as to what position they should take regarding the proposed strike, some taking the position that it was only a palliative at best, that it was not worth such a gigantic struggle as must be engaged in, if it was to succeed.

Following is part of an interview by Albert R. Parsons printed in the *Chicago Daily News*, March 13, 1886:

> The movement to reduce the work-hours is intended by its projectors to give a peaceful solution to the difficulties between the capitalists and laborers. I have always held that there were two ways to settle this trouble, either by peaceable means or violent methods. Reduced hours, or eight-hours, is the peace-offering. Fewer hours mean more pay. Reduced hours is the only measure of economic reform which consults the interests of the laborers as consumers. Now, this means a higher standard of living for the producers, which can only be acquired by possessing and consuming a larger share of their own product. This would diminish the profits of the labor exploiters.

The Central Labor Union of Chicago, consisting of 25,000 German trades unionists, passed a resolution, requesting August Spies, editor of the *Arbeiter-Zeitung* (German daily), and Albert R. Parsons, editor of *The Alarm* (English weekly), to advocate in their paper and speeches, the eight-hour day. This settled the controversy: Parsons, Spies and all the active revolutionary spirits in Chicago went to work in earnest. The result of their activities was made manifest, for when the first of May, 1886 arrived, it found Chicago the best organized city in America. In this city the working class struck between 50,000 and 60,000 strong and tied up the city more completely than I have ever seen it tied up during the thirty years that I have been a resident here.

On the afternoon of May 3rd, there were large numbers of strikers in the Southwestern portion of Chicago, among them the McCormick Reaper Works' employees. According to the capitalist papers there was rioting among them. The police were called out to quell the riots. As is usually the case, when the police were called out, the working people were sticking together in large numbers; [though the police] did manage to quell some of them. On this occasion, they shot seven working men and clubbed many hundreds unmercifully.

The next evening the Haymarket meeting was called. The Haymarket meeting is referred to historically as the "The Haymarket Anarchists' Riot." There was *no riot* at Haymarket except a police riot.

Mayor Carter Harrison attended the Haymarket meeting, and took the stand at the Anarchist trial for the defense, not for the state. The Mayor testified that he attended the Haymarket meeting as the highest peace official in Chicago for the purpose of dispersing it, should it require his attentions as such. The Mayor further testified that when the meeting was about to be adjourned, he went to the Desplaines Street police station, and ordered the inspector to send his reserves to their several beats as the meeting was adjourning, was peaceable, and that he the Mayor was on his way home. No sooner was the Mayor out of sight, than the inspector, who wished to do something officious at the time of the great strike, rushed a company of police upon the meeting that had practically adjourned. At the onrush of the police, someone threw a bomb. Who threw that bomb, no one to this day knows, save he who threw it. He has never been found.

But the capitalist class didn't care whether they found the bomb thrower or not; what they wanted was the leaders of the great strike, to get them out of the way and to frighten the slaves back to work. And the scheme worked magnificently, for after the bomb was thrown, the slaves for the most part forgot they had a grievance. Of course, to give the barest outline of the trial and death of my husband and comrades, would make this letter entirely too long. But the key to why their lives were sacrificed is found in the following excerpts from State's Attorney Grinnell's address to the jury. He said:

> Gentlemen of the jury, these defendants at the bar are not more guilty than the thousands who follow them. They have been selected and indicted by the grand jury because they are leaders, convict them and save our society.

The great strike of May 1886, was an historic event of great importance, inasmuch as it was, in the first place, the first time that workers themselves had attempted to get a shorter work day by united, simultaneous action. To be sure there had been some earlier agitation, but always among the politicians in legislative halls and in congress. Needless to say such agitation was of no avail. But this strike was the first in the nature of Direct Action on a large scale, the first in America. It had its lasting effects, because it broke through the stone wall of the long-hour custom. What was gained by the workers was never wholly lost. The hours of labor have never been as long, as a whole, since 1886, as they were before that time.

Of course the eight-hour day is as antiquated as the craft unions themselves. Today, we should be agitating for a five-hour work day, or six at the most, but the IWW, I presume, has taken up the eight-hour cause on the principle that we must not get too far away from those we wish to influence or our labors are wasted.

The worldwide unrest among the wage class is the most hopeful sign of the times. Labor is learning that its most powerful and effective weapon is in its muscles and its brains. Let it withdraw these and the capitalist system is paralyzed. What labor wants is land for the landless, produce to the producer, tools to the toiler and death to wage-slavery.

> *Thine oppressor's hand recoils,*
> *When thou, weary of thy toil,*
> *Shun'st thy plough, thy task begun,*
> *When thou speak'st: Enough is done.* *

Industrial Worker, May 1, 1912

STRAY THOUGHTS ON MAY DAY

May 1st has marked a time in the long procession of the centuries. The beautiful month of May, when all nature emerges from her long, dreary, winter's sleep. Beautiful month of springtime and flowers. Man, too, revives his hopes and renews his resolves, for he, also, feels the flood-tide of nature in his own being and responds as best he can to her charming voice.

What more appropriate time could the workers choose to renew their efforts to inaugurate a better day, a better life for themselves? I noticed that this grand old International Day was more widely observed this year than has been the case in recent years.

The papers tell us of its observance both in America and Europe on an extensive scale. I was in Cleveland on May 1st and witnessed a fine demonstration by Socialists, on the Public Square; the speeches were fine and appropriate.

Well, I am on another trip through the East, however, I shall not go farther East than Ohio this time. I find organized labor somewhat in the position of Mr McCawber, Esq., "waiting for something to turn up."*

The Agitator, June 1, 1912

THE ELEVENTH OF NOVEMBER, 1887
Introduction to *Famous Speeches*
of the Eight Chicago Anarchists

The Eleventh of November has become a day of international importance, cherished in the hearts of all true lovers of liberty as a day of martyrdom. On this day were offered upon the cruel gallows-tree, martyrs as true to their high ideals as were ever sacrificed in any age.

The writer will assume that the present generation is but superficially informed regarding the details that led up to the eleventh of November, for in this busy age, twenty-five years is a long time to remember the details of any event, however important.

In 1886 the working class of America, for the first time, struck for the reduction of the hours of daily toil to eight per day. It was a great strike. Chicago was the storm-center of that strike, because of the activities of the martyrs of the eleventh of November, 1887.

The working class practically tied up the city of Chicago, Illinois, for three days. On the afternoon of May 3rd, of that year, the police shot several strikers and clubbed many more brutally. The next evening, May 4th, the now historic Haymarket meeting was held. The Haymarket meeting is referred to historically as the "Haymarket Riot." This Haymarket meeting was absolutely peaceable and quiet. The Mayor of Chicago attended the meeting, and subsequently took the stand as the first witness for the defense at the Anarchist Trial, so-called. Following is the mayor's testimony in part:

> I went to the meeting for the purpose of dispersing it, in case I should feel it necessary for the safety of the city. There was no suggestion made by either of the speakers looking toward calling for immediate use of force or violence towards any persons that night; if there had been, I should have dispersed them at once. I went to the police station during Parsons' speech and I stated to Captain Bonfield that I thought the speeches were about over; that nothing had occurred or looked likely to occur to require interference, and that he had better issue orders to his reserves at the stations to go home. Bonfield replied that he had reached the same conclusion from reports brought to him. During my attendance I saw no weapons at all upon any person. In listening to the speeches, I concluded that it was not an organization to destroy property. After listening a little longer, I went home.

This extract is here given from the Mayor's testimony, because this meeting is referred to very often, even by radicals, as the "Haymarket Riot."

Had the inspector of police obeyed the Mayor's orders and not rushed a company of police upon that peaceful meeting, there would have been no trouble. Instead, as soon as the Mayor left, the inspector rushed a company of bluecoats to the meeting; they began clubbing the men and women and scattered them in every direction. Upon this onrush of the police, someone threw a bomb. Who threw that bomb, no one to this day knows, except he who threw it.

The bomber has never been identified, never been arrested, consequently could never have been tried, but my husband and his comrades were put to death on November 11th as co-conspirators with the bomb-thrower, but *he* is unknown!

Our comrades were not murdered by the state because they had any connection with the bomb-throwing, but because they had been active in organizing the wage-slaves of America.

The capitalistic class didn't want to find the bomb-thrower; they foolishly believed that by putting to death the active spirits of the labor movement of that time they could frighten the working class back into slavery.

The so-called trial was the greatest travesty upon justice of modern times. The bailiff who was selecting the jury, a creature named Ryce, boasted thus:

> I am managing this case and I know what I am about. Those fellows
> are going to hang as certain as death. I am calling such men as the
> defendants will have to challenge peremptorily and waste their time
> and challenges. Then they will have to take such jurymen as the
> prosecution wants."

The jury that did try the case was out less than three hours. They
left the court room after four o'clock on August 23 and before seven
o'clock the self-same afternoon had reached the astounding verdict,
sending seven men to the gallows and the eighth man to the penitentiary for the term of fifteen years. The trial had lasted some sixty-
three days. Think of the massive testimony that the jury would have
had to go over in order to give them even the semblance of a fair
trial! Then think of the audacity of a jury being out less than three
hours, and of the brutality of a community putting men to death
under such a verdict and never allowing them a new trial!

Albert R. Parsons, my husband, never was *arrested*. On May 5,
the day after the Haymarket meeting, when he saw the men with
whom he had been organizing labor for the past ten years of his life,
being arrested and thrown into prison and treated generally as criminals, he left Chicago. On June 21, the day the trial began, he
walked into the courtroom, unrecognized by the police and detectives, and *surrendered* himself, having been indicted during his
absence and a reward of $5,000 having been offered for his arrest.
He asked the court to grant him a fair trial that he might prove his
absolute innocence. He was never granted the shadow of a fair and
impartial trial and was put to death with the rest of his comrades on
November 11, 1887!

The men were asked if they had anything to say as to why
sentence of death should not be passed upon them. They arose in the
court room on the days of October 7, 8 and 9, 1886, and delivered
their now so "Famous Speeches," giving their reasons why the
sentence of death should be suspended and they be given a new
trial. They called the judge's attention to the fact that the leading
capitalistic paper in Chicago had opened up its columns to receive
subscriptions to a fund of $100,000.00, to be paid to the jury as a
present for the verdict it had rendered against them. But they were
never granted a new trial. They were, instead, railroaded to the

gallows at the command of the money power!

For the past two years I have devoted myself to selling their speeches. The Seventh Edition, of 14,000 will be out in a few weeks' time, being now in press. These copies of the Speeches have been practically all sold amongst the members of the conservative organized labor unions. The Jewish comrades now have a movement started to have these Speeches translated and published in the Yiddish language.

Verily, their "SILENCE IS MORE POWERFUL THAN THE VOICES THAT WERE STRANGLED" that dark November day!

There could be no other results in a matter that had already been fixed in advance, except such as came on October 10, when the infamous Judge Jeffreys* gave out his reasons for denying a new trial, and afterwards sentenced them to death. No more remarkable scene than that could well be imagined. The hot, stifling courtroom, crammed to its utmost capacity by an eager crowd, quite in sympathy with the capitalistic ideas and breaking at times into clapping, which was silly and hypocritically repressed by the only too gratified court—the little, ugly, hard-visaged judge, with a nutcracker bald head and cunning eyes. One could fancy his tender mercies, if ever they existed, as dried up and long since fallen to dust. Then the coarse, brutal state's attorney, with the ferocious howl of an infuriated, blood-hungry wild beast, who continually bellowed for the lives of these men before him. And the little cunning, red-headed lawyer who made the most telling speech that the State gave out, a cruel, crafty effort that misrepresented everything, absolutely, and did it so foxily that each point drew blood like the slash of a claw.

Forever will live in the minds' eye of those who had the sad privilege of seeing this strange and terrible scene, the calm and noble countenances of the accused, who showed no feeling except when an occasional flicker of fine scorn passed over their refined countenances, as they sat and heard their every act, deed, thought, meaning, however innocent, misrepresented, twisted and their lives going to certain destruction at the hands of their enemies' tools and minions. All the way through and especially noticeable the last day, detectives and police, plain-clothes men, and others of that ilk, filled the court room. When the sentence of death was being pronounced, these fellows stood up and pointed their revolvers right into the faces of our comrades, evidently fearing—scoundrels are ever cowards—an attempt at rescue on the part of friends, on this, the last appearance of the prisoners outside of the jail. But no such attempt was made and sentence was passed, the date of the execution being set for December 3. One instant to give a passing hand-shake to sorrowing relatives and indignant friends and they were marched back again to their dungeons.

Then began the long, tedious period that lasted for over a year, our comrades languishing in their living tombs. The attorneys for the defense began occupying themselves with their preparations for taking the case to the Illinois Supreme Court and accordingly an appeal was made to a judge of that body, on November 25, who granted a supersedeas and admitted that error had been made. Many friends believed that this meant that our comrades would evidently walk out free men, but those who had seen the working of the trial knew better. They knew that the supersedeas as well as every other step of the proceedings, was carefully taken with a view to giving the world an idea of the "impartiality" of the absolutely hellish conspiracy, the animus of which was to do away with certain labor leaders whose intelligence, honesty and fearlessness had made them objects of the fear and hatred of the capitalistic "Robber-Baron" element.

This supersedeas, therefore, merely gave a breathing spell for the lawyers to get ready their briefs for a hearing of the plea for a new trial before the Illinois Supreme Court. The friends and many persons, indignant at the monstrousness of proceedings they had only supposed possible under the reign of the "Little Father" of all the Russians, were firmly determined to try every court available, in order to prove and make the point that the courts were not impartial but, instead, the ready tools of the moneyed power. Our comrades themselves always believed this, that no justice would ever be done them by any court, and, indeed, that the whole affair was to be regarded in the light of a howling farce, were not murder, of the most revolting and cold-blooded sort, the evident intention.

This appeal went to the Illinois Supreme Court on March 18, had the same hypocritical examination, the honorable judges deciding that no errors had been made of any gravity—when, as a matter of fact, they were there thick—and the decision of the lower court was sustained, the day of execution being again set, this time for November 11, 1887.

So month after month dragged along for our comrades, suffering acutely for want of exercise and fresh air—when this old jail was subsequently torn down to make way for the new one, a black lake of putrid filth was found, fully explaining why our comrades had their teeth decay and fall out—and in the frantic efforts of friends, sympathizers and enlightened persons generally, to show the mass of the people what was being done, all in the name of law and order, the relatives, friends, the Defense Committee and many persons of recognized position—writers, lecturers, and poets—held meetings, distributed circulars, brochures and wrote articles for the radical press—the capitalistic press was solidly closed against one word of the truth—and the public would have finally seen at least something of what was being done, had not the police, ever vigilant in their hate, counteracted it all by "finding" bombs at regular intervals, under sidewalks, in alleys, etc. Made by the police themselves, placed there in the night, these bombs were solemnly "found" in the morning and served as the subject of blazing editorials and solemn, life-sized pictures in the leading capitalistic papers. The public, which does not go below the surface, believed what it was told.

The old, wicked Judge "Jeffreys," the State's Attorney, and other tools of the money-power, all whined about threats on their lives and so on, and so the public was kept at that excited and ugly temper that was wanted of them—as when, two thousand years ago they shouted "Let loose to us Barabbas"—for the hirelings of the high and mighty scoundrels who were putting through this judicial murder fully meant to so befuddle the public on the facts as to get its backing and consent.

So the time wore away through the hot summer to autumn, when the attorneys for the defense took the case to the U.S. Supreme Court. These scoundrelly bigwigs, in solemn conclave, decided that no Constitutional right had been violated, although two of the main points in the Constitution had been grossly trodden under foot, namely, the right of free speech and free assembly at the Haymarket meeting, and the right to free and impartial trial at the hands of the law, which was absolutely wanting. It is a matter of conjecture as to how many millions of capitalistic gold went to animate that

146

decision!

So we are brought down to the last days when the friends and sympathizers circulated petitions for executive clemency by the thousands and the police, no less active, "found" bombs and even one of the Supreme Court judges got an infernal machine (which turned out to be a box of papers about some other case!). The only serene people were our condemned comrades. Finally, at the last hour, an appeal was to be made to the governor for executive clemency. This meant a sort of pilgrimage to the City of Springfield by hundreds of persons, including scores of friends and some of the relatives. Thousands of others wrote letters; our comrades themselves—except in the cases of Fielden and Schwab*—positively refusing to admit that they had committed any misdemeanor or to ask for any mercy. They protested that they wished merely justice. The city was, at this point, in a perfect state of martial law. Several regiments were camped, with cannon, close to the city hall, and sleuths, armed police and such wretches were everywhere. One wondered why the plutocrats were so afraid of their bad consciences which, doubtless, raised avenging hands from every shadow!

Our comrades, in the meantime, were subjected to every outrage and humiliation. Their clothing and even their persons were continually searched, the daily papers were denied them, they were no longer allowed the freedom of the corridors for a moment's exercise, relatives and friends no longer admitted to see them. They were even forced to the horrid task of willing their bodies, each separately to their families, to keep them from being desecrated by the police, after death.

The weather had turned very cold and those of the members of the families who had not gone to Springfield to see the governor gathered in a pitiful group in the corridor of the jail vestibule, really then the court house, and beginning in the early morning, begged for a last word of farewell with their loved ones. This was flatly denied. All the livelong, terrible day these people, mostly women, had to stand on their feet in the bitter cold and witness the preparations for the execution—they had seen the coffins carried in the evening before!—without either food or water, hour after hour, with a brutal crowd of police and their friends crowding about to the extent of hundreds, staring and commenting. At midnight, a very few of the relatives were taken in, one at a time, by a turnkey, with a lantern in his left hand and a revolver in the other. The inside of the jail buzzed like a hive, so full was it with reporters, police, sleuths, and other tools of the moneyed class.

After a few seconds of agonized parting, each poor woman was marched back and left in the dark corridor. After midnight, the "decision" of the governor was not announced in order to keep down any attempt at rescue by friends and sympathizers. The governor simply refused interference, except in the cases of Schwab and Fielden, who received life-sentences in the penitentiary (afterwards, these were pardoned by Governor Altgeld).

The morning of the eleventh found our dear comrades composed, smiling, firm without bravado. I, who had been denied admission on Thursday evening, went again in the morning, accompanied by a woman friend and comrade and our two children, to say a last farewell to my beloved husband and that the children might have their father's blessing and last remembrance.

A cordon of police armed with Winchesters surrounded the jail. Pressing against this was a crowd of thousands of persons. To one policeman after another I appealed without effect, until one told us to come around the corner and he would "let us in," which he proceeded to do by hustling us into a patrol wagon and taking us to the station house, where we were stripped naked, searched and locked up all day, until three in the afternoon, that is three hours after the execution. The city was in the hands of the people and drunken police. The rich, to a man, had gone away for a few days' vacation, terrorized by their own black consciences.

The execution itself was put through as swiftly as possible. Our comrades were not to be permitted the usual speeches, always accorded to doomed men. They had, however, foreseen this and each had prepared a sentence to express his last feelings. This they said just as the caps were being adjusted that forever shut the light from their eyes. Their clear voices rang out in those sentences now become classics. Let us pass over the agonizing scenes at the homes of the men, when wives, children, mothers, sisters, brothers, friends, received back the bodies of their dear ones, from whom life had been crushed out and all only because they had dared to tell the workers the simple truth!

On Sunday morning, November 14, the funeral took place, and no more remarkable sight will ever be witnessed than that procession of countless thousands that filed past the dead as they lay in their homes, and then the procession of five black hearses that passed through the city, accompanied by bands playing dirges and carriages bearing the friends and sympathizers, the mourners directly behind the hearses. Past the offices of the newspapers that Parsons and Spies had edited, to the Northwestern train in waiting, passed the cortege which bore them to Waldheim Cemetery. The streets along which this remarkable procession wended its way were solidly packed with human faces and as the hearses passed, hats were taken off by thousands, instinctively, as it were. They did not know it, but they somehow felt that they were in the presence of great dead who had died nobly!

At the cemetery, a way had to be cleared through the dense throng for the procession. Four addresses were made in English and German, the most notable being the oration pronounced by Captain Black, leading attorney for the defense. And so, beneath mountains of floral offerings, before sorrowing relatives and friends, all that was left of our beloved comrades was consigned to their last resting place, on the banks of the Des Plaines River.

But only their ashes, for their noble, true souls, animated by an undying faith in and love of humanity, will never die and their last words will continue to echo in the hearts of people, down through the ages of men, who still believe in rights and the brotherhood of man. That the present generation thinks this may be gathered by the fact that on every Decoration Day, or day set apart for the decoration of the graves of soldiers that died in our wars, thousands pass around the Anarchist Monument in silent homage or grave thoughtfulness, as if weighing the question of these men "who were not as other men."

The Famous Speeches of the Eight Chicago Anarchists,
Twenty-Fifth Anniversary Souvenir Edition,1912

JUST A FEW STRAY OBSERVATIONS
on "Political" Socialism, War, and the State

Scientific socialism (so-called) has been taught in Germany for more than fifty years. The State scientists abjured the tenet "Father, Son and Holy Ghost" but took, in its stead the text: "Workers of all countries, unite!" This beautiful bit of phraseology "was glimmering" when the political representatives of "science" (backed by more than four million voters) helped their imperial master lay a war levy of a billion marks or more for the prosecution of a war on workers of other countries.

And each of the scientists was honored by a clasp of the imperial hand to the tune of "Deutschland Uber Alles!" German scientific Socialism has stifled the revolutionary tendency, once so promising.

* * *

Can governmentalists ever reach the limit in the matter of invasion? If so, this must be the limit: It seems that the Chicago women who apply for municipal employment are subjected to a physical examination as to their chastity, the results of these inquisitions being duly recorded by the attending clerk. The *Chicago Herald* makes editorial comment as follows:

Civil Service Indignities: The indignities to which young women seeking positions as nurses in the schools and at the municipal tuberculosis sanitarium were subject deserve condemnation in the highest degree. According to civilized law even a person accused of a crime is presumed to be innocent until proved guilty. The burden of proof is on the prosecution. The accused is not required to establish his innocence.
The nurses subjected to the physical examination prescribed by the city civil service commission's medical examiner were called on to prove their innocence. The suggestion of such an examination was degrading; its infliction was a gross insult.

* * *

Could wars ever be carried on were it not for that institutionalized credulity which manifests in reliance upon "The State?" Our socialist friends often say: "We see Anarchism gets you nowhere." Where did "scientific" political socialism get the millions of socialists in Europe? Frankly, could Europe be worse cursed than it is if

there had never been a single speech delivered by a political socialist or a book written by one of them? Really, could it be worse?

Instead of a Magazine,
September 1915

WORKERS AND WAR

T he anti-military spirit which is developing among the masses
of Europe will tell the governments of the Earth that the
workers have no trouble that needs to be settled by cruel war;
and if the rulers have trouble, they can settle them by fighting it out
among themselves. The working class wants to enjoy the fruits of
their toil, the short time they journey this Earth. But we are told that
kind of talk is unpatriotic, that every man ought to be willing to
fight for his country. What country belongs to the wage class?

The Agitator, February 12, 1917

MELVILLE STONE'S LIES

February 27, 1922

E ditor, Federated Press: I read Mr Stone's article on the Chicago anarchists published in *Collier's Weekly* of February 5,
1922, and consider it so defective in so many ways that it's
absolutely unreliable as a historical document.* He not only lies
about Mr Schilling, whom he accuses of being a part of the revolutionary anarchist groups, but he also lies about Mr Parsons and
myself when he says that it was understood that he (Stone) was to

have the privilege of surrendering my husband to the court when he voluntarily returned to be tried. It is true that Mr Stone sent for us and offered me a substantial monetary consideration, if such a privilege were granted him. I reported his request to Capt. William P. Black, the leading counsel of the defendants, who at once turned it down, and no one ever went near Mr Stone afterwards.

There isn't any doubt in my mind but what his other statement about Mr Schilling reporting to him from time to time about the "impending revolution" is just as false as his statement that Mr Schilling was connected with the revolutionary groups.

Yours very truly,
Lucy E. Parsons,
3130 N. Troy St.

Copy in Ashbaugh papers,
Charles H. Kerr Company Archives,
The Newberry Library, Chicago

LETTER TO EUGENE V. DEBS

March 12, 1926

Grand Old Rebel! I am writing you these few lines to express my admiration and appreciation of the grand stand that you have taken, regarding your restoration to citizenship. Why should you ask for that which you, in justice and fairness, have never forfeited? It is [thanks] to such characters as you that reaction is halted and this stupid old world moves on a little, until the time for change is reached.

I am sending you a copy of the *Life* of my late husband, Albert R. Parsons, also a copy of the *Famous Speeches*. You will observe in reading his *Life* that he too refused to ask for a "pardon," stating that he would not ask for pardon for that which he had not forfeited—his life. If you mention these books in the *Appeal*, *Life of Parsons* is $3.25; *Speeches*, $1.25.

Hoping that your useful life may be spared for many years, I am Sincerely yours,

Lucy E. Parsons

From *Letters of Eugene V. Debs,*
J. Robert Constantine, ed. Volume 3, 1919-1926.
(Urbana: University of Illinois Press, 1990)

WHO WERE THE PIONEERS
OF THE EIGHT-HOUR DAY?

D oes this rising generation know that those who inaugurated the eight-hour day were put to death at the command of capital?

Until forty years ago men, women and children toiled ten and often twelve hours a day in factories for a mere pittance, and children from six to nine years of age had to work to help keep up the family.

The Knights of Labor, a powerful organization claiming 500,000 members, had never agitated for a reduction of the hours of labor. Then who were the pioneers of the eight-hour movement? Those martyrs who were strung from the gallows in Chicago on November 11, 1887, the much-lied-about and abused Anarchists.

I will verify this statement. Until 1885 there had never been a concerted action for the reduction of the hours of labor. If eight hours was mentioned in some of our meetings (they were never really mentioned), why, that was only a dream to be indulged in by fools; the bosses would never tolerate such a thing, was the reply.

In 1885 a convention was held in Chicago, composed largely of delegates from Canada. They passed a resolution calling upon the workers of this country and Canada to unite in a demand for a reduction of the hours of toil to eight a day on the first of May,

1886, and to strike wherever it was refused.

Albert R. Parsons brought the matter up before the Trade and Labor Assembly of Chicago, the first central labor body ever organized in this city, a body which he himself organized and of which he was elected president three consecutive times. The matter was hotly debated and finally rejected on the ground that the bosses would never tolerate it.

The Central Labor Union, composed of German mechanics, took the matter up and endorsed it. At the same time they passed a resolution requesting August Spies, editor of the Chicago *Arbeiterzeitung*, the daily German paper, and Albert R. Parsons, editor of the *Alarm*, to support it in their papers and speeches; they were both splendid orators.

Thus it was that the eight-hour movement got under way. Many other cities agitated for it, but Chicago was the storm center of the movement, owing to the zeal and courage of the men and women of this city who worked day and night for it. The result was that when May 1st, 1886, arrived, it found Chicago well-organized and demanding the eight-hour day, striking by the thousands where the demand was refused. It was a veritable holiday for the workers.

The bosses were taken completely by surprise. Some were frightened and threatening; some were signing up; others were abusing those "scoundrels" who had brought all this trouble upon "our" city, and declaring that they would be made examples of, that they ought to be hung and the like.

The police were unspeakably brutal, clubbing and shooting; factory whistles blew, but few responded.

I was chairman of the Women's Organization Committee and know personally how that great strike spread. I have never seen such solidarity.

Rest, comrades, rest. All the tomorrows are yours!

Labor Defender, November 1926 (excerpts);
original title, "The Haymarket Martyrs"

I'LL BE DAMNED IF I GO BACK TO WORK
UNDER THOSE CONDITIONS!
A May Day Speech

I am greatly afraid, Comrades, that my voice will not reach to all of you, but believe me that my spirit will reach to the farthest corners of the room.

I have spoken in this hall before, and in other halls, and one wish I have always wished, that the architect who built a hall like this—with the acoustics that this hall has—would never build another one like it.

Now, I am going to bring you a message, that forty-four years ago today we had our first introduction on American soil of what was known as a great strike. It was the introduction of the eight-hour day in America. From twelve hours to eight hours was a great step, and I have the honor to be one of those who was so instrumental in my small and humble way in preparing for that immense strike.

I have been in the labor movement for many years. I have been in the labor movement since I was a mere girl like these kids I see today. When I saw these little girls with their bright eyes and forward-looking movements, and how bright and happy they were, I went back through all those years and pictured myself, and I said, after forty-four years I see these children who are going to come and take the place of those like myself who will some day, and very soon, of course, pass away. But these will carry on the great fight until the last battle has been fought and won.

I wish I had the strength. I wish I had the wisdom. I wish I was a fine enough speaker to depict to you Chicago forty-four years ago. In my humble way I will try to give you just an outline of it. We had been organizing the working class for nearly a year. Very quietly. They were so downtrodden in those days that the capitalists paid little attention to them, but when the first of May came, and this slogan went forward, "Throw down your arms, throw down your tools and come out," why, I have never seen such a strike. It was a psychological moment. It was a spontaneous strike, and they came out by the thousands until the capitalist class claimed themselves there were forty thousand who stood out in the streets of Chicago, and when they tried to get them back to work, [replied] "I will be damned if I go back to work under such conditions."

That was the spirit of that day. That was the dividing line between the long- and the short-hour movement in America. From that day on—there are unions in this city today who were organized then; the bakers union, and other unions. And they have never gone back to the old time. If it had not been for the organization that came into existence just on the heels of this—our leaders were put to death, and after they were put to death there came to the front an organization, a so-called labor organization, the AFL, the American Federation of Labor. What have they to produce? What have they to show for their forty-six years? They have gone together and scraped together the mechanics, two million in a population of thirty-eight million. They have two million under their banner. The others can go straight to hell for all they care, they are nothing but the common herd.

As I see this movement today, forty-four years from now will tell a different story. Forty-four years from now I believe such a thing will have disappeared. It will have disappeared from the face of the Earth, because I see in this movement today—I have seen many movements come and go. I belonged to all of those movements. I was a delegate that organized the Industrial Workers of the World. I carried a card in the old Socialist Party. And I am now today connected with the Communists [through the International Labor Defense]. So I have seen these movements come and go.

In human affairs, in life, it is just as the ebb and flow of nature. It is like the ebb and flow along the ocean's way, along the shore of the seaside. Those waves come and play their part and go, but they all leave their imprint, until the ocean itself is worn away with time. And so no one need be discouraged because these waves of human forces to the radical movement come and go. They all leave their imprint. The radical imprint, they all leave something behind, and the next great movement like this one that comes, simply steps into the footsteps of those who have gone, and carry it further until the emancipation comes. It is a lesson of history. We do not accomplish all in one day, or one generation. It goes on to the other generations, and I believe, without flattering this organization, that they have the right dope. I can't help but believe they will go on and on, and will not pass away like the other organizations, because I think they have the substantiality.

Now, I am not going to speak a great while. I want to tell you something about the Haymarket, and then probably I am about through. The movement of 1886, the eight-hour movement was a grand success. For a few days they had the capitalists on the run, you might say. They were taken completely by surprise. We had a great movement trial at that time, and I must, right here and now, I must put in a slight protest for the so-called anarchists in those days. I am an anarchist: I have no apology to make to a single man, woman or child, because I am an anarchist, because anarchism carries the very germ of liberty in its womb.

Now, we anarchists and others of us here, we carried on this strike. We carried on this movement, and on the third of May—I want to tell you now something you can carry home that will be substantial—on the third of May the McCormick Reaper Works people struck and came out to demand the reduction of hours of daily toil from twelve to ten. They did not even ask for eight hours. That was beyond their reckoning. And on that day the great monstrous meeting was being held, the police went down to that meeting, and they shot and clubbed those innocent people, and the next day the Haymarket meeting was called as a protest against the clubbing and shooting of those people on the day before.

It was a conspiracy of the capitalist class to break up the great movement that was sweeping everything before it. And so this Haymarket was nothing in the world but a conspiracy of the capitalist class to break up the movement of that time. It was a police riot. We were as quiet and peaceful as you sitting here today. But it had its effect. We have always believed it was a detective that threw that bomb in the Haymarket for the purpose of breaking up the eight-hour movement. Now, beware such scoundrels in your midst. As you go on, they will put up some job like that on you. We know they are capable of doing any kind of work. We believe that bomb was thrown by some detective. The man who threw the bomb at the Haymarket was never known. I am not here to give you a speech on the Haymarket. It was only a great labor movement.

I want you to take it home that the men lying sleeping in the

Waldheim Cemetery were simply martyrs to the labor movement. Those of you today who enjoy better conditions, we must enjoy better conditions after forty-four years, there is no such thing as standing still in the world, nowhere in nature, so there has to be some better—today the Communists are demanding six hours or seven hours, rather. Forty-four years from now, and a long time before that time, four hours and even less they will demand, until there isn't one man or woman in the world who wants to work who cannot get it. That is the kind of movement of the future.

That will not be all. If that is the case, Capitalism will have gone by the board. I do not expect to live that long, but I do believe when I see young people and earnest people who will drop their work in times like this, when work is so scarce, come out in the mid-week and defy the capitalist classes, and come out in the sunlight, and show them as standing solid for shorter hours and better conditions, that *that* means earnest people and those are the kind of people we have got to have.

The Communist Party has hundreds and hundreds in prison cells. They are there, and before I am through I am going to ask you to send one mighty shout to them of encouragement, that we are supporting them. I will have that in a moment. Now, Comrades, go on with the movement, carry it on, carry it through, because the Comrade has said here, they call us Reds. I don't know that *that* is very bad. I do not believe that is a very bad name. We are pretty red. I tell you I am a real Red. The scarlet flag (holding up scarlet cloth).

The workers' flag is deepest red,
  It shrouded oft our martyred dead;
And 'ere their limbs grew pale and cold,
  Their life-blood dyed its every fold.

Then raise the scarlet standard high,
  Beneath its folds we'll live and die.
Though cowards flinch, and traitors sneer,
  We'll keep the red flag flying here. *

We make the fight of ages. It is the flag, and that flag shall fly above the ramparts of capitalism throughout the world, and no woman will be compelled to sell the hallowed name of virtue for a piece of bread. No child will be compelled to go in our factories.

No man walking the earth asking for bread that cannot get it. It will wave up above the ramparts of capitalism. Then hail the banner of the workers, the red flag throughout the world.

Today we march, we send our greeting upon ocean's waves, we send them continent to continent, we send our friends across the ocean and all climes and countries: We are with you. Our hearts throb. The working class throughout the world, proclaim the doom of capitalism and wage-slavery.

I have asked the permission of the chair just a moment, I have said something to you about the Haymarket, I haven't said much about it, and I have brought with me the speeches that were delivered by our comrades, my husband and his comrades, and I wish to say to you that *that* red flag, that they were shrouded in the red flag, and they lie in their last resting place enfolded in the red flag. But these are the speeches. When they were sentenced to death they were asked if they had anything to say why sentence of death should not be passed upon them. They arose in the court room, and for three days they delivered these masterful speeches.

There has nothing been added of a fundamental nature to the labor movement in those forty-four years. You wonder how those men of that day could have such a grasp of the labor movement. For three days they said to the court, they said, "Honorable Judge" —my husband said,

> Honorable Judge, we are not delivering these speeches either to you or to your class. When we are dead and gone, to which we believe we are doomed, this is our message to the world and the working class to know why we were put to death. All these years of my life I have been carrying this message to you, the working class.

Should any of you wish to read these speeches, they have the cuts of the five martyrs. They are here in the hall. I thank you.

Chicago, May 1, 1930; from the transcript

Lucy Parsons, 1920

U.S. ANARCHISM IN THE 1930s:

Chicago, February 27, 1934

Dear Carl: Your letter of February 13 was quite a surprise and illuminating, to learn that you had arrived at the same conclusions that I had some years ago: that is, that Anarchism has not produced any organized ability in the present generation, only a few little loose, struggling groups, scattered over this vast country, that come together in "conferences" occasionally, talk to each other, then go home. Then we never hear from them again until another conference is held. Do you call this a movement? You speak of "the movement" in your letter. Where is it? You say, "I just feel disgusted." I have been for a long time.

Anarchists are good at showing the shortcomings of others' organizations. But what have they done in the last fifty years, you say. Nothing to build up a movement; they are mere pipe-dreamers dreaming. Consequently, Anarchism doesn't appeal to the public. This busy, practical world cares nothing for fine-spun theories—they want facts, and too, they want a few examples shown.

They talk about cooperation. You state that you have been trying to get the four little excuses for papers to cooperate to get out one worthwhile publication, but you can't succeed. . . .

Anarchism is a dead issue in American life today. Radicalism has been blotted off the map of Europe. The Vienna horror-slaughter is too shocking to realize. The worker is a mere appendage to the capitalist factory. Machinery has eliminated him. Robert Burns said: "O God, that men should be so cheap, and bread should be so dear!"

Radicalism is at a low ebb today. We are living in strange times! Despotism is on horseback, riding at high speed. The worker is helpless; he has no voice in his mode or method of life—he just floats along on the tides of ill times. I went to work for the International Labor Defense (ILD) because I wanted to do a little something to help defend the victims of capitalism who got into trouble, and not always be talking, talking, talking. When the little work that is now being doled out [is finally doled out], what then?

As ever, fraternally, yours

Lucy E. Parsons

Copy in Ashbaugh Papers,
Charles H. Kerr Company Archives,
The Newberry Library. Chicago

LETTER TO TOM MOONEY

June 11, 1936

Dear Comrade Tom Mooney: I received your most welcome letter some days ago and would have replied sooner but was not well.

Regarding the data of the trial, I sent about all I had on hand to universities.

I mailed you a copy of *The Life of Albert R. Parsons*. It contains much valuable information which you wished. I am sending under another cover copies of the *Alarm* that Parsons published. In your lonely prison cell, it will take you back to other days of our movement.

Well, dear Comrade, I have been very active in your cause, to liberate you; have spoken in many meetings both here and in the east. I am not discouraged in the belief that justice will be done you, and that I can clasp your hand a free comrade—vindicated!

My vision is becoming so dim that it is difficult for me to write legibly any more.

I am yours fraternally,

Lucy E. Parsons

Copy in Ashbaugh Papers,
Charles H. Kerr Company Archives,
The Newberry Library. Chicago

ON A NEW BIOGRAPHY OF ALBERT PARSONS

September 24, 1937

I have read the manuscript of your forthcoming book on Albert R. Parsons and the early labor movement in Chicago. The manuscript shows painstaking care, and elucidation so much needed for the enlightenment of this generation.

Of course the part that interested me most was your description of the Haymarket meeting, the trial so-called, and the death of the martyrs, November 11, 1887.

You have dug beneath the mountain of lies that has been heaped upon my husband and his comrades these fifty fleeting years, and without any attempt at "over" writing, have given the bare, cold facts, taken from the record, and proving that they were innocent of any bomb-throwing, and were simply lynched!—to satisfy a howling mob of greedy capitalists, who would not be satisfied with less than their lives, who somehow thought by hanging those labor leaders they could crush the labor movement. "What fools these mortals be."

They have always tried to crush the labor movement in this way, but in vain. Eugene Victor Debs was imprisoned because he dared to raise his voice against the war craze of the capitalists in 1914. There was Big Bill Haywood, who had to flee the country of his birth and die in the land of promise—Soviet Russia. Then there is Tom Mooney, pining away his valuable life behind prison bars because the rich utility barons demand it. On "Memorial Day" of this year the bosses and police repeated what they had done fifty years ago—they killed four workers, and wounded many others, at the Republic Steel Corporation plant in south Chicago. . . .

I hope and believe your book will have a wide circulation; appearing as it will on the eve of the fiftieth anniversary of the martyrdom of the Chicago Labor leaders will lend great interest; besides, there is so much fine labor history in it that this generation should know.

Excerpts from a letter to Alan Calmer,
published as the Foreword to Calmer's book,
Labor Agitator (New York, 1937)

NOVEMBER 11: FIFTY YEARS AGO

Once again on November 11, a memorial meeting will be held to commemorate the death of the Chicago Haymarket martyrs—1937 is the fiftieth anniversary and this meeting bids fair to be more widely observed than any of the forty-nine previous ones. It has taken fifty years to dig the facts of this case out from under the mountains of lies that were heaped upon our martyrs by the exploiters in their attempt to cover up their crime of sending five labor leaders to the gallows.

You will hear people say today, as one said to me recently, "What! Calling those Haymarket bomb-throwers martyrs? Do you think I believe that? You will have to show me." Now I am writing this article to "show" all such doubting Thomases.

The Haymarket meeting was held as a protest against the brutality of the police who, during the great strike for the eight-hour work day of 1886, tried with all the vicious power at their command to defeat the hopes of the workers.

At noon on May 3, 1886, the striking workers of the McCormick Reaper Works were discussing their problems in a mass meeting near the plant when two patrol wagons loaded with policemen appeared. With drawn clubs the police rushed down upon the workers, clubbing them. Two workers were shot [and killed].

The next evening the famous Haymarket meeting was held to protest against this and other outrages of the police. This meeting was attended by about 3,000 people, men and women. I myself was there with our two children.

The meeting was perfectly peaceful, but when it was about to adjourn a company of police charged upon it and ordered the crowd to disperse. At the onrush of these police, violators of the law they were sworn to uphold, someone—to this day he is unknown—hurled a bomb into the ranks of the police. Then hell broke loose!

The papers came out next morning with great flare headlines: "The anarchist dynamiters, bomb-throwers had started a riot and had intended to blow up the city; and but for the courage of the police they would have thrown many more bombs," and so on. They demanded that the leaders be arrested and made examples of.

Six weeks later eight men (our Chicago martyrs) were arraigned in a prejudiced court before a prejudiced judge and a packed jury. They were charged with murder.

Mayor Harrison of Chicago testified for the defense. Here are a few lines from his testimony:

I went to the meeting for the purpose of dispersing it should it require my attention...when the meeting was about to adjourn I went to the station (about half a block away) and told Captain Bonfield to send his reserves home, that the meeting was about to adjourn, that the speeches were tame.

But State's Attorney Grinnell, pointing to the defendants, said "These defendants are not more guilty than the thousands who follow them; they were selected by the grand jury because they were leaders. Convict them and save our society."

Bailiff Rylance was heard to remark: "I am managing this case. These fellows will hang as sure as death. I am selecting men [for the jury] that will compel the defense to waste their challenges; then they will have to take such men as the prosecution wants."

The trial, so-called, lasted sixty-three days. The jury brought in a verdict of guilty in three hours.

The judge, in dismissing the jury-men, thanked them for the verdict and told them that carriages were outside to take them home. The capitalists were overjoyed. A sum of $100,000 was paid the jury. The *Chicago Tribune* on August 20 opened its columns thus: "The twelve good men and true have rendered a just verdict, let them be generously remembered. Raise a sum of $100,000 to be paid with the thanks of a grateful public."

When the march to the gallows was begun, all the men showed remarkable courage without the slightest tinge of bravado. Parsons was wonderfully composed. The moment his feet touched the gallows he seemed to lose his identity. "No tragedian ever made a more marvelous presentation of a self-chosen part," a capitalist paper reported.

On that gloomy morning of November 11, 1887, I took our two little children to the jail to bid my beloved husband farewell. I found the jail roped off with heavy cables. Policemen with pistols walked in the enclosure.

I asked them to allow us to go to our loved one before they murdered him. They said nothing.

Then I said, "Let these children bid their father good-bye, let them receive his blessing. They can do no harm."

In a few minutes a patrol wagon drove up and we were locked up in a police station while the hellish deed was done.

Oh, Misery, I have drunk thy cup of sorrow to its dregs but I am still a rebel.

One Big Union Monthly, November 1937

MESSAGE TO THE IWW'S
GENERAL DEFENSE COMMITTEE

> Chicago 12/22/37
> General Defence Committee
> A Happy New year to you
> all and many more of
> them to you all.
> yours for Industrial
> Freedom
>   Lucy E Parsons

Chicago, 12/22/37

General Defense Committee: A Happy New Year to you all and
many more of them to you all.
    Yours for Industrial Freedom,
      Lucy E. Parsons

Original letter in the personal archives
of Carlos Cortez, Chicago

NOTES TO THE TEXTS

Page 56. Joseph Labadie (1850-1923) was a prominent labor organizer and editor, union printer, and philosophical anarchist; an especially vocal defender of the Haymarket Eight. His collection of labor and radical papers grew into the Labadie Collection at the University of Michigan at Ann Arbor—one of the best repositories of such literature in the world.

Page 58. Hugh O. Pentecost, of Newark, was one of the few clergymen who protested the unjust trial of the Haymarket anarchists, though he later turned against them.

Page 74. "Teddy" was Theodore Roosevelt, twenty-sixth president of the U.S., noted for his white supremacist, imperialist, anti-immigrant, anti-labor policies.

Page 89. C. L. James, of Eau Claire, Wisconsin, was a well-respected anarchist in the late nineteenth century, author of a book on the French Revolution and other works.

Page 99. Alton B. Parker (1852-1926) was chief justice of the New York court of appeals (1898-1904) and candidate of conservative Democrats for the U.S. presidency in 1904.

Page 118. John M. O'Neill was a member of the Western Federation of Miners executive board and editor of the union's official organ, the *Miners' Magazine,*

Page 122. Lucy's harsh criticism of the IWW's first year, under the ineffectual administration of Charles O. Sherman, was shared by most IWW militants.

Page 130. "Another Orchard" refers to Harry Orchard, the notorious paid perjurer hired by the Pinkerton Detective Agency to testify against Haywood *et al*.

Page 135. The Japanese martyrs included the well-known anarchist Kotoku (who had met with anarchists and IWWs in the U.S.) and eleven others who were charged with "High Treason" in 1910 and executed in 1911. Their frame-up trial was markedly similar to the Haymarket trial.

Page 140. The quoted lines are from the poem, "Bread and Freedom," by the German lyric poet Georg Friedrich Herwegh (1817-1875), a friend of Karl Marx. On October 8, 1886, Albert Parsons began his final speech to the court with this poem.

Page 141. Mr Micawber is a character in Charles Dickens's novel *David Copperfield.*

Page 144. Here Lucy likens Judge Gary to George Jeffreys (1644-1689), Lord chief justice and chancellor under James II in England, a judge noted for his injustice and brutality.

Page 147. Fielden and Schwab appealed to Governor Oglesby for commutation.

Page 151. In his later years, ashamed of his role in the Haymarket Red Scare and frame-up, *Chicago Daily News* owner Melville Stone tried to bill himself as a hero in the case, while slandering George Schilling. The latter, a major figure in the Chicago labor movement, was a friend of Albert and Lucy Parsons, although he did not share their anarchist views.

Page 158. The transcriber of this speech garbled these lyrics, which are corrected here. Written by Jim Connell in London, 1889, "The Red Flag" was one of the most popular songs in the IWW's Little Red Song Book.

Haymarket Centennial poster by Carlos Cortez (1986)

ROXANNE DUNBAR-ORTIZ

AFTERWORD

"One Infallible, Unchangeable Motto: Freedom" Reflections on the Anarchism of Lucy Parsons

L
ucy Parsons's personae and historical role provide material for the makings of a truly exemplary figure—not to mention a "poster girl"—for U.S. radical history. Think of it: lifelong anarchist, labor organizer, writer, editor, publisher, and dynamic speaker, a woman of color of mixed black, Mexican, and Native American heritage, founder in the 1880s of the Chicago Working Women's Union that organized garment workers and called for equal pay for equal work, and also invited housewives to join with the demand of wages for housework—and later (1905), co-founder of the Industrial Workers of the World (IWW), which made organizing women and people of color a priority.

But acknowledgment of Lucy Parsons has been minimal.

It is not that radical women have been ignored in the new women's history, or that women have been ignored in the new histories of radicalism; witness the prominence in both of other female activists of the time: Voltairine de Cleyre, Emma Goldman, Mother Jones, Ida B. Wells, Mary Marcy, Elizabeth Gurley Flynn, Agnes Smedley, Margaret Sanger, Jane Addams, Dorothy Day, Mabel Dodge, Helen Keller, Kate Richards O'Hare, Carolyn Lowe, and many others are presented as strong and autonomous activists. Certainly, as Carolyn Ashbaugh, Parsons's lone biographer, asserts, "Lucy Parsons was black, a woman, and working class—three reasons people are often excluded from history."

On the left, the view of Lucy Parsons as the "devoted assistant" of her martyred husband Albert Richard Parsons is prevalent. Feminists who have forgotten the radical working class roots of the feminist movement have also overlooked Lucy Parsons. Editors of the Radcliffe *Notable American Women* three-volume work consigned Lucy Parsons to their discard file on the grounds that she was "largely propelled by husband's fate" and was "a pathetic figure, living in the past and crying injustice after the Haymarket Police Riot".[1]

169

The present publication of Parsons's selected writings and speeches surely illustrates the fallacy of such a characterization of the fifty-plus years of her life as anarchist, agitator, publicist, and organizer which followed the 1887 judicial murder of her partner, Albert Parsons. And Lucy Parsons did not become an activist only the day after her husband's death. Indeed, she "was a recognized leader of the predominately white male working class movement in Chicago long before the 1886 police riot."[2] The Working Women's Union predated the death of Albert Parsons by nearly a decade. Most trade unions of the time did not allow female membership but pressure from the Working Women's Union opened up the Knights of Labor to women.

Dismissal of Lucy Parsons as a serious subject of U.S. radicalism is not new. In her own time it seems she was regarded by some, such as Emma Goldman, as a ubiquitous nuisance, using her dead husband's martyrdom and name to gain attention and remain in the spotlight. Undoubtedly, Parsons did use her status as martyr's widow to gain the platform she aggressively pursued until her death to promote revolutionary consciousness and action, based on anarchist and workingclass principles. Goldman lumped Parsons with wives of "anarchists [who] marry women who are millions of miles removed from their ideas . . . even Lucy Parsons, who goes with every gang proclaiming itself revolutionary."[3]

Goldman had to know better. One suspects competition for celebrity. Not until the advent of the radical wing of the Women's Liberation Movement in the late 1960s, did feminist theory forge a new debate by asserting that female human beings constitute a caste/class in all human societies, historically and contemporaneously.[4] Up to that development, female activists tended to adopt male leadership methods and personae, even when their constituency or audience was primarily female. Leadership style and even the necessity for leadership at all—generally termed "elitism"- were fiercely debated in the radical movements of the 1960s. Being a female agitator in the limelight in Lucy Parsons's time was a rare occurrence with probably no more than ten percent of the ranks of the anarchist and socialist movements being women and even less in positions of leadership. Goldman, surely in part due to her long exile during which she was neither organizing nor in touch with ordinary workers, developed ideas which struck Parsons as foolish and unrealistic. However, even more than two decades before being exiled from the United States, Goldman was in a very different position than Lucy Parsons. Ashbaugh writes:

> Emma Goldman spent a year on Blackwell Island in 1893-94 for inciting to riot. After her release, she went to Europe to study nursing and midwifery and returned to the U.S. in the fall of 1896 to become the anarchists' foremost advocate of free love. Goldman could study in Europe and travel in educated circles, opportunities which Lucy Parsons's dark skin precluded for her. Goldman became interested in the freedom of the individual; Parsons remained committed to the freedom of the working class from capitalism.[5]

This and other theoretical issues marked early leftist thinking on the "woman question," as it was then called. Whereas Sixties feminists who advocated woman freeing herself sexually drew upon Goldman's life and work as a model, the socialist-feminists of the same period did not "discover" Lucy Parsons. Their differences, which may be gleaned from their separate writings and work, touched on the issues that became key to later feminist theory. With the internationalization of the woman question during three decades of United Nations' sponsored activities and education, these issues are quite contemporary and probably more important than ever in terms of developing universalist theory upon which to visualize and build a just and equitable social order.

Historian Alice Echols lists some of the unresolved questions debated by female radicals in the Women's Liberation Movement:

> Was women's behavior the result of conditioning or material necessity? Was heterosexuality a crucial bargaining chip in women's struggle for liberation (as in "a revolutionary in every bedroom cannot fail to shake up the status quo") or a source of women's oppression? Should women's sexual pleasure be enhanced or men's sexuality curbed? If the personal was political, was the political personal? Did men oppress women because of the material benefits they reaped or because they found it intrinsically pleasurable to do so? There was even some disagreement on the question of whether radical feminism implied the minimization or maximization of gender differences.[6]

Goldman and Parsons had in common a commitment to the working class and to the destruction of capitalism and the state. They each also maintained a lifelong eschewal of liberalism, particularly electoral politics—even before women had the vote—since, they believed, the whole structure and grid of society must be destroyed and rebuilt. What these two female giants of the U.S. anarchist movement did dispute was sexual behavior, marriage, and family. Ashbaugh observes that while Emma Goldman, and the anarchist movement as a whole, moved toward sexual freedom and individualism, Lucy Parsons tended toward what became the Socialist Party and the Industrial Workers of the World—that is, toward mass action, revolutionary industrial unionism, and anarcho-syndicalism.[7] Ashbaugh makes a critical distinction between the two world-views:

> Radical feminism was a workingclass development which came out of the analysis of the role of women under capitalism. Lucy Parsons's feminism, which analyzed women's oppression as a function of capitalism, was founded on working class values.
>
> Emma Goldman's feminism took on an abstract character of freedom for women in all things, in all times, and in all places; her feminism became separate from its working class origins. Goldman represented the feminism being advocated in the anarchist movement of the 1890s. The intellectual anarchists questioned Lucy Parsons about her attitudes on the women's question. . . . For her, the women's question was part of the class question.

Yet, Lucy Parsons posed a question that hardly echoes traditional family values: "How many women do you think would submit to marriage-slavery if it were not for wage-slavery?"[8]

And Lucy Parsons never put family before principles. A dramatic case in point occurred when her eighteen-year-old son enlisted to serve in the Spanish-American War. Actively opposed herself, as a militant anti-imperialist, she had him committed to a mental institution. Apparently, the boy was "normal" by society's standards but not by the standards of Lucy Parsons's political principles. Albert Parsons, Jr. died in the asylum two decades later without ever being seen by his mother during that time.[9]

The distinction between Goldman and Parsons in the prioritization of the woman question preshadows the disagreement between radical and socialist feminists of the 1960s women's movement, the anarchist/radical feminist holding that destroying capitalism is necessary but not sufficient for female liberation, and the socialist/communist feminist believing that the establishment of socialism will automatically destroy the basis for women's oppression. (Analogous questions also arose in the radical movements of

172

African-Americans, Chicanos, and Native Americans.) What is particularly significant about the debate in the earlier period, in contrast with more recent times, is that these discussions took place within the workingclass movement. That fact might suggest that we rethink the basis of similar debates in the Sixties women's liberation movement, that were widely attributed to the middle-class backgrounds of the female activists who promoted an autonomous women's liberation movement.

Ashbaugh oversimplifies Parsons's views on marriage, monogamy, the family, and free love, when she characterizes them as traditional and conservative:

> The women's question was a real problem for Lucy. She had three strikes against her from birth: poor, non-white, woman. She felt poverty the most acutely, and she put the fight against racism and sexism secondary to class struggle. She believed in monogamous marriage and the nuclear family as fundamental "natural" principles and argued that the problems of marriage resulted from the economic system, not from flaws in the institution itself.[10]

Parsons worried, as did some radical feminist theorists of the Sixties movement, that obliterating those values and institutions under capitalism would harm women, not men.[11] In other words, Parsons was not a utopianist, but she did advocate that women free themselves from the kitchen and the nursery and be economically independent of men if possible.

Above all, Lucy Parsons defended female workers, including their right to the same pay as male workers. At the founding convention of the Industrial Workers of the World in 1905, Lucy Parsons made it clear that she saw her presence and voice as representing women: "We, the women of this country, have no ballot even if we wished to use it . . . but we have our labor . . . Wherever wages are to be reduced the capitalist class uses women to reduce them." She did not forget the particularities of the oppression of women within the working class itself. On the question of dues, she referred to low-paid women textile-workers and wanted assurance that dues be set at an amount that would allow them to join the IWW:

> They are the class we want. This organization is for the purpose of helping all, and certainly it is the women in the textile mills that are

173

the lowest paid...Make it so that the women who get such poor pay should not be assessed as much as the men who get higher pay.[12]

Regarding free love, Parsons was concerned about venereal disease and pregnancy as well as the fate of the children born of such unions, the burden of which would inevitably reside with the woman. Parsons did argue that prostitution and rape could and did happen within marriage but did not fault the nuclear family as an institution inherently oppressive to women. At any rate, it was clear to her that for the working class, the family was its sole refuge. Parsons herself never remarried but did have a number of serious relationships with men, which is a statement in itself from one who so firmly embraced "direct action" and "propaganda by the deed."

Emma Goldman did not reconsider Lucy Parsons's concerns later on when she passed middle age and found that men were no longer attracted to her sexually, whereas older men, including her own lifetime companion Alexander Berkman, had no problem attracting young women. In 1936, Goldman expressed her outrage at this double standard:

> I do not believe that middle-aged women lose their sexual attraction or "usefulness," as you call it. That is only one of the many prejudices in regard to women. I know scores of women who are wonderfully youthful, vivacious, and interesting who are past middle age. It is only the idiotic discrimination society makes between the man and woman of the same age. Thus any man, no matter how decrepit, can and does attract young girls. Why should it not be the same in the case of the woman?[13]

Lucy Parsons was not alone in the anarchist movement of the time in questioning the extension of human freedom to sexual promiscuity and the end of monogamous relationships. In fact, there is little in Lucy Parsons's life and work that would suggest, as Ashbaugh does, that Parsons was not truly an anarchist. For reasons that are not clear, Ashbaugh insists that Lucy Parsons was not authentically an anarchist, and inexplicably encloses the term itself in quotation marks:

> Lucy Parsons had claimed to be an "anarchist" when the title was pinned on her by the bourgeois press and her state-socialist enemies. She believed her husband had died for anarchism, and she was prepared to defend and die for anarchism. Although her beliefs were syndicalist rather than anarchist, she tried to cling to the "anarchist" movement as it changed shape.[14]

Although Ashbaugh's entire thesis in her biography rests on arguing and demonstrating that Lucy Parsons was her own person as an activist, here she falls into the living-for-her-husband theme. She appears to be trying to rescue Lucy Parsons's "image" with this absurd assertion. A few years before her death, during the Franklin Roosevelt era, Parsons worked in the International Labor Defense (ILD) and was therefore close to people in the U.S. Communist Party, which always downplayed Parsons's anarchism. Ashbaugh seems to have fallen into the same mode, revealing her own lack of respect for anarchism as a revolutionary current as varied as socialism or communism. Anarcho-syndicalism, which promoted federation through trade unions and workplaces, and projected the general strike as a revolutionary strategy, was one of several prominent theoretical lines in the anarchist movement. Anarcho-pacifism sought to create autonomous communities and non-violent resistance; anarcho-individualism promoted the absolute freedom of the individual; anarcho-mutualism envisaged federalist networking of autonomous group cooperatives; and anarcho-communism rejected wages, advocated armed struggle, called for free communal associations sharing according to need from community-based distribution centers.[15]

None of these variants of anarchism were mutually exclusive, and they overlapped each other. Certainly, Lucy Parsons embraced direct action and even armed struggle as viable and admissible means of struggle, which would make her as much anarcho-communist as syndicalist.

In terms of armed self-defense on the part of the oppressed, there can be no doubt as to Parsons's thinking. While denying Parsons's real commitment to anarchism, Ashbaugh documents evidence of it even before Albert Parsons's death. In Lucy Parsons's 1884 article, "To Tramps," she tells of advising a tramp who was about to commit suicide that he should use explosives and take a few rich people along: "Each of you hungry tramps who read these lines, avail yourselves of those little methods of warfare which Science has placed in the hands of the poor man—*Learn the Use of Explosives!*" Ashbaugh warns that this essay "has frequently been used out of context to do a disservice to her and her cause." But Lucy Parsons's own statement makes such an apology dubious. Ashbaugh further apologizes for Parsons's militancy, explaining why Lucy Parsons was more committed to "propaganda by the deed" than her husband: "all the oppression which Lucy suffered for her dark skin and her womanhood went into the anger with which she encouraged the use of dynamite."[16]

"To Tramps" was typical rather than exceptional in Lucy Parsons's writings and speeches. In some of her writings she argued that destruction of ruling-class property was educational and liberating for workers, energizing their struggles under horrible conditions. Here, she sounds like a precursor of Frantz Fanon, who proposed that violence was not only necessary but liberating to oppressed peoples in throwing off the shackles of colonialism.[17] Lucy Parsons, and most anarchists, regarded the new invention, dynamite, as an almost magical tool, easily accessible to workers. Parsons wrote, "The voice of dynamite is the voice of force, the only voice which tyranny has ever been able to understand. It takes no great rummage through musty pages of history to demonstrate this fact." During the same year, in reaction to militia shooting and killing of workers in Illinois, she called for nothing less than "a war of extermination and without pity" against the wealthy. Soon her group resolved "to arm and organize into a company and become a part of the military organization now forming throughout the city" and "to establish a school on chemistry where the manufacture and use of explosives would be taught." She advised a black community in Mississippi to respond to recent white supremacist massacres of their friends and families that

> You are not absolutely defenseless. For the torch of the incendiary, which has been known to show murderers and tyrants the danger line, beyond which they may not venture with impunity, cannot be wrested from you.[18]

In Lucy Parsons's view, fomenting chaos in the ruling class, the people becoming ungovernable, destruction of the institutions and rulers of government, not to be replaced, were positive anarchist goals, not ones born of exhaustion and hopelessness. As a matter of fact, many anarchists, including Goldman and Parsons, moderated, not their ultimate goals of stateless societies, but violence as a means, in the wake of the demise of left hegemony in the working class in the face of Fascism and Nazism. However, Lucy Parsons never agreed that there was any need for centralized political and economic authority other than to protect the rich and exploit the propertyless.

One contemporary praised Parsons, comparing her to French anarchist Louise Michel, famous as a leader of the 1871 Paris Commune: "She is a wonderfully strong writer and it is said she can excel her husband in making a fiery speech." Albert Parsons was widely considered just about the best English-speaking orator the working class had. Once he was silenced by imprisonment, Lucy Parsons's already finely developed organizing skills and voice expanded and refocused; she continued to speak for anarchism and the need for revolutionary organization as well as on such topics as "The French Revolution" and "The Paris Commune," but she also emphasized the defense of political prisoners, a cause she worked for tirelessly during the following fifty years of her life.

Lucy Parsons used her platform as the wife of Albert Parsons to support the Haymarket defendants, and after their deaths used her platform as the martyr's widow to memorialize them, all the while promoting anarchist goals and methods. Never did she moderate her views in order to win public support. The main issue at the mass protest meeting that ended in the Haymarket police riot was police brutality against workers striking for the eight-hour day—a struggle Lucy Parsons supported. She made it clear, however, that she envisaged a time when working hours would be reduced to one or two.

All through the "Red Scare" that followed the Haymarket bomb incident, she continued to uphold the right of workers to defend themselves against police or military attack. "For five years, I have spoken against this civilization. . .! have said that any and all means are justifiable to destroy it, and by that statement I will stand or fall. . ."[19] In her speeches, Parsons argued that the Haymarket bomb had been placed by goons of Wall Street in order to destroy the eight-hour movement. She said that those conspirators were the same ones who drove poor women into prostitution and working men to drink and suicide.

> I come to talk to you of those who stand in the shadow of their own scaffolds. I come to you an avowed Anarchist. I am a revolutionist, but I incite no one to riot, for I am not out on that mission; I hope to be some day. . . .[20]

The birth of the Industrial Workers of the World gave Lucy

Parsons an ideal vehicle for fusing her anarchist and syndicalist views. Although there is no indication that she had a hand in writing the IWW constitution, its Preamble captures her unshakeable anarchism and class perspective:

> The working class and the employing class have nothing in common. There can be no peace so long as hunger and want are found among millions of working people and the few, who make up the employing class, have all the good things of life.
> Between these two classes a struggle must go on until the workers of the world organize as a class, take possession of the earth and the machinery of production, and abolish the wage system. . . .

Lucy Parsons was not only an ornament, sitting on the platform with Eugene V. Debs and Mother Jones as Big Bill Haywood gave the opening speech of the 1905 founding meeting of the IWW. When she addressed the convention, Parsons made it clear that she was present among the many representatives of organizations of anarchists, syndicalists, socialists, and trade unionists, not as a representative of a particular organization, but as a representative of the most oppressed of humanity: child laborers and working women, including prostitutes—arguing that a revolution based on the needs and participation of the most oppressed would benefit all workers rather than creating a workers' elite.

In that speech and during the proceedings, Parsons strenuously argued in favor of the most fundamental of anarchistic demands: the general strike as the primary tactic of a revolutionary strategy to crush the power structures, and the non-electoral politics characteristic of the IWW as an organization. She wove these two concepts together elegantly in her speech:

> My conception of the strike of the future is not to strike and go out and starve, but to strike and remain in and take possession of the necessary property of production. . . Do you think the capitalists will allow you to vote away their property? You may, but I do not believe it. . . It means a revolution that shall turn all these things over...to the wealth producers. . . When your new economic organization shall declare as brothers and sisters that you are determined that you possess these things, then there is no army that is large enough to overcome you, for you yourselves constitute the army.[21]

As Phillip S. Foner wrote: "In the IWW, the general strike was first mentioned at the founding convention where it was advocated by Lucy E. Parsons. . . . But the majority of the delegates were not prepared to endorse a general strike, and the proposals died for lack of support."[22]

Following the convention, Lucy Parsons became editor of an IWW-oriented newspaper: *The Liberator*, that she herself named in honor of the abolitionist newspaper founded by William Lloyd Garrison. While agitating for the new union through the newspaper, she also remained a militant activist. Eight years after its founding, the IWW began to focus on organizing the unemployed, starting on the west coast. Among her many activities, the most publicized nationally occurred in San Francisco in 1914. The IWW had begun to focus on organizing the unemployed and started on the west coast. Parsons, representing the IWW, led a march and demonstration of unemployed men. The police attacked the marchers, and Parsons was arrested.[23]

U.S. entrance into World War One brought intense political repression against all "reds," especially the IWW. Hundreds of its most active members were railroaded to prison, and for a time the union was severely weakened. Much like the late twentieth and early twenty-first century, the 1920s was a lonely and frightening time to be a social activist. But Lucy Parsons was not one to retire from activism. Despite her advanced years and poor eyesight, she continued to speak on May Day and November 11th meetings, and to work with such groups as the IWW's General Defense Committee and the Communists' International Labor Defense to secure the freedom of such political prisoners as Tom Mooney and the Scottsboro Eight. She gave as her reason for working with the Communist Party: "They are the only bunch who are making a vigorous protest against the present horrible conditions."[24]

In her 1955 memoir of the years 1906-1926, Elizabeth Gurley Flynn, who became a leader of the Communist Party, draws a picture of Lucy Parsons as an iconic, devoted old widow woman:

> I remember Mrs Parsons speaking warmly to the young people, warning us of the seriousness of the struggles ahead that could lead to jail and death before victory was won. For years she traveled from city to city, knocking on the doors of local unions and telling the story of the Chicago trial. . . .[25]

How a dark-skinned single woman managed to survive the life of an open revolutionary during that period is phenomenal. For Lucy

Parsons, identity—other than being of and for the working class—was irrelevant.

Yet the ethnic/racial identity of Lucy Parsons was an issue to others during her own life and remains disputed. Ashbaugh began her biography with an unequivocal characterization: "Lucy Parsons was black, a woman, and working class."[26] On the other hand, Hedda Garza in *Latinas: Hispanic Women in the United States*, began a four page snapshot of Lucy Parsons quite differently but also unequivocally:

> Born in 1853 in Johnson County, Texas, Lucia Eldine Gonzalez never discussed her family background except to say that she was Mexican. Throughout her life, though, dark-complexioned "Lucy" (as her friends called her) was often referred to as "that colored woman" by her enemies.[27]

Chicano historians Afredo Mirande and Evangelina Enriquez devoted a section to Parsons in their *La Chicana*, as did Rodolfo Acuna in *Occupied America*. These historians proudly present Parsons as a Chicana by birth and a great labor activist, but they point out that beyond claiming to be Mexican, she seems to have had no relationship with the Mexican community or labor movements of the time.[28] Chicano and Mexican labor movements were continuous during Parsons's active life and were closely linked to the organizations with which she was affiliated: the anarchist movement, the IWW, and the International Labor Defense, and very active in her home state of Texas. This was the time before, during, and in the wake of the Mexican Revolution. Therefore, it does seem odd that if Parsons was certain and proud of her Mexican heritage—and claimed a Spanish maiden name, Gonzalez—that she would not take a greater interest in the grand historical drama of her people being played out before her eyes.

Ashbaugh leans toward the theory that Lucy Parsons was actually African-American, and perhaps born into slavery. Parsons denied being black and until recently has not figured into African-American historical revisions. Ashbaugh observes that Lucy Parsons internalized the racism of white society to the extent that she denied her own black ancestry, and that her denial of being black, and therefore oppressed as a black woman, limited her ability to analyze her social position, or that of oppressed peoples in general, in relation to anything but class status. Parsons did speak on the question of race, always maintaining, as she did regarding women, that the oppression of African-Americans was economically based. Following the 1886 massacre of thirteen black people in Jim Crow Mississippi, Parsons wrote an article titled, "The Negro. Let Him Leave Politics to the Politician and Prayers to the Preacher." She asked:

> Are there any so stupid as to believe these outrages have been, are being and will be heaped upon the Negro because he is black? Not at all. It is because he is poor. It is because he is dependent. Because he is poorer as a class than his white wage-slave brother of the North.[29]

And yet, Lucy Parsons's April 1892 response to southern lynchings would suggest a more complex theory than mere reductionist economism.[30] These texts have a familiar ring to us, permeated as they are with the language of self-reliance and self-determination—the language of Malcolm X and the Black Panthers, challenging the civil rights movement during the 1960s.

Whatever her national identity or her position on the woman question, Lucy Parsons was without doubt a highly visible labor leader for over seventy years, a time stretching from just after the end of the Civil War to U.S. entrance into World War Two. In view of her role in the Knights of Labor, the Working Women's Union, the eight-hour struggle, and the IWW, the fact that Parsons is little mentioned in revisionist labor studies as a militant in her own right is truly inexplicable.[31]

If a person's politics can be at least in part judged by her library, then Lucy Parsons was no professional widow of a radical martyr. At her death at the age of eighty-nine, she owned more than 1500 books on the topics of sex, socialism, and anarchism—all of which, along with all her papers, were stolen by the FBI or the Chicago Red Squad and never seen again.[32]

Sadly, Lucy Parsons and her grand legacy of revolt and revolution fell into the cracks of radical, labor, feminist, African-American, Latino, and Native American revisions of history, an orphan in memory as well as in life. Heroes are selected by states to promote patriotism, so it is no surprise that Lucy Parsons is absent there. But heroes are selected by revolutionary movements as models of tireless commitment and struggle under conditions of great adversity, human and flawed, often damaged human beings who overcome their vulnerabilities through their struggles on behalf of all oppressed and exploited persons, groups, and peoples.

The absence of Lucy Parsons's ideas and life work has been a great loss for generations of radicals during the second half of the twentieth century and the beginning of the twenty-first. *Direct action*, however—the best two-word summary of Lucy Parsons's anarchist activism—has made a big comeback, and will continue to be relevant in the coming years, as evidenced in the many ongoing anti-WTO, anti-World-Bank, and similar demonstrations all over the world. With their colorful diversity and improvisation, these mass protests remind us of the revolutionary parades led by Lucy Parsons in the 1880s.

For a better understanding of the concept of direct action, and its implications, no other historical figure can match the lessons provided by Lucy Parsons.

San Francisco, October 2003

NOTES

1. Carolyn Ashbaugh, *Lucy Parsons; American Revolutionary*. Chicago: Charles H. Kerr Publishing Company, 1976: 6.   2. Ashbaugh, 6.

3. Letter from Emma Goldman to Alexander Berkman, January 1932, Paris, in Richard and Anna Maria Drinnon, eds. *Nowhere at Home*. New York: Schocken Books, 1975.

4. See Shulamith Firestone, *Dialectic of Sex*. New York: William Morrow, 1970; Roxanne Dunbar, "Female Liberation as the Basis of Social Liberation," in Robin Morgan, ed.. *Sisterhood is Powerful*. New York: Vintage, 1970.

5. Ashbaugh, 200.

6. Alice Echols, *Daring to be Bad: Radical Feminism in America, 1967-1975*. Minneapolis: University of Minnesota Press, 1989: 6.

7. Ashbaugh, 200.   8. Ashbaugh, 202.   9. Ashbaugh, 208-209   10. Ashbaugh, 201.

11. One of the original radical women's liberation groups of the late 1960s, "Redstockings," debated the same issue extensively and in depth, publishing much of their thinking. One of the groups' founders, Kathy (Amatnik) Sarachild, argued that "most women wouldn't join a movement that called for free love...because they know that isn't freedom for women or love for women." She proposed, suggesting an analogy to Marxist-Leninist theory, that women "use marriage as the 'dictatorship of the proletariat' in the family revolution. When male supremacy is completely eliminated, marriage, like the state, will disappear." Echols, 145-46.

12. Ashbaugh, 217-18.

13. Letter from Emma Goldman to Ben Taylor, in Drinnon, 121. Goldman never regretted living the risky and painful life of a free woman: "Of course the price we modern women and men too pay for our own development and growth is very great and painful, but one must go ahead or remain in the dull state of the cow...There is nothing without a price and we must be ready to pay it." Letter from Emma Goldman to Alexander Berkman, in Drinnon, 134.
     One of the celebrities of the 1960s women's liberation movement, Germaine Greer, author of the best-selling *The Female Eunuch*, was the darling of male-dominated press and public. By all contemporary western standards, Greer was a beautiful, sexy woman, and she was proud of it. She set out to demonstrate, along with Gloria Steinem, that a feminist need not fit the dreary stereotype. Two decades later, Greer—much like Goldman—raged over her treatment at midlife in *The Change: Women, Aging and the Menopause* (Alfred A. Knopf, 1991). Like Goldman, Greer does not regret her freedom, but does condemn the stark, male supremacist, double standard disgust for older women as sexual beings. *The Change* was not a best-selling book.

14. Ashbaugh, 201

15. Juan Gómez-Quinones, *Sembradores Ricardo Flores Magon y El Partido Liberal Mexicano: A Eulogy and Critique*. Los Angeles: University of California Chicano Studies Center, Aztlan Publications, Monograph No. 5, 1973: 6.

16. Ashbaugh, 55.

17. Frantz Fanon, *Les damnés de la terre*. Paris: Francois Maspero, editeur, 1961; English edition. *The Wretched of the Earth*. New York: Evergreen, 1968.

18. Ashbaugh, 57-60, 66.   19. Ibid., 107   20. Ibid., 110   21. Ibid., 217.

22. *The Industrial Workers of the World, 1905-1917. Volume IV: History of the Labor Movement in the United States*. New York: International Publishers, 1965: 140.

23. Foner, 137-38.   24. Ashbaugh, 254, 255.

25. Elizabeth Gurley Flynn, *Rebel Girl: An Autobiography. My First Life (1906-1926)*. New York: International Publishers, 1955: 79.

26. Ashbaugh, 6.

27. Hedda Garza, *Latinas: Hispanic Women in the United States*, New York: Franklin Watts, 1994: 34.

28. *La Chicana: The Mexican-American Woman*. Chicago: University of Chicago Press, 1979: 86-95; *Occupied America: A History of Chicanos*. New York: Harper Collins, 1988: 151.

29. Ashbaugh, 66.   30. In *Freedom*. April 1892.

31. One history of the radical labor movement in the U.S. devotes four pages to a section titled "Mr. and Mrs. Parsons." It deals with Lucy as an activist in her own right, but it is as though she died when Albert Parsons was executed because she is never mentioned again in the text. Richard O. Boyer and Herbert M. Morais, *Labor's Untold Story*. New York: United Electrical, Radio and Machine Workers of America (UE), 1955, 1973: 84-87. However, Phillip S. Foner in his history of the I.W.W. briefly, highlights Parsons's autonomous and active role two decades after Albert Parsons' execution.   32. Ashbaugh, 261.

In jail, January 1915

183

Books for an Endangered Planet

WALLS & BARS: Prisons & Prison Life in the "Land of the Free" by Eugene V. Debs; Introduction by David Dellinger. Both memoir & critique, this is one of the most insightful books ever written on prisons, by one of the most influential & best-loved radicals in U.S. history. *Revolutionary Classics*. 264 pages. $16.00

LABOR STRUGGLES IN THE DEEP SOUTH & Other Writings by Covington Hall, edited & introduced by David R. Roediger. This beautifully illustrated first-hand account describes many of the finest hours of integrated unionism in the U.S. & the IWW's role in creating unity across racial lines. 272 pages. $14.00

COLD CHICAGO: A Haymarket Fable by Warren Leming, with illustrations by Carlos Cortez. A play in cabaret form with original music. *"Warren Leming's play on the Haymarket affair is the best antidote we have for the National Alzheimer's —our forgetfulness of yesterday"* —Studs Terkel. 112 pages. $15.00

WHERE ARE THE VOICES? & Other Wobbly Poems by Carlos Cortez, with twenty illustrations by the author, including linocut portraits of Lucy Parsons, Joe Hill, Ricardo Flores Magon, & others. Introduction by Archie Green. 64 pps. $10.00

THE STORY OF MARY MACLANE & Other Writings by Mary MacLane, introduced by Penelope Rosemont. An audacious teenager's memoir, the publishing scandal of 1902. Reviews by Clarence Darrow & Harriet Monroe. 218 pp. $15.00

WE WILL RETURN IN THE WHIRLWIND: Black Radical Organizing, 1960–1975, by Muhammad Ahmad, national field chairman of the Revolutionary Action Movement and founder of the African People's Party. Introduction by John Bracey. 340 pages. $18.00

JUICE IS STRANGER THAN FRICTION: Selected Writings of T-Bone Slim, edited & introduced by Franklin Rosemont. The IWW's greatest "Man of Letters" was an outstanding humorist, a wordplay genius, a presurrealist. *"T-Bone Slim has a lot to tell us, and does it well"* —Noam Chomsky. 160 pages. $10.00

ACCEPTABLE MEN: Life in the Largest Steel Mill in the World, a Memoir, by Noel Ignatiev. A first hand account of everyday white supremacy, patriarchy, and the exploitation of labor, but also on-the-job resistance. 110 pages. $12.00

PRAISE BOSS! The Erotic Adventures of Mr. Block, a play by Joseph Grim Feinberg. The subject of Joe Hill's eponymous song and Ernest Riebe's cartoons, Mr. Block is the working class's biggest blockhead. 105 pages. $10.00

CHARLES H. KERR

Est. 1886 / 8901 South Exchange Avenue, Chicago, Illinois 60617